MORE SACRED COWS

By the same author:

INSECT INVADER

SCIENCE IS A SACRED COW

More Sacred Cows

LITTLE HERESIES IN
AMERICA AND ELSEWHERE

Anthony Standen

WILLIAM MORROW AND COMPANY
NEW YORK, 1962

To Lisl with Love

Contents

Introduction

YEARS AGO I read Ruth Benedict's *Patterns of Culture.* This wonderful book describes three cultures: the Zuñi Indians, who lead quiet lives, largely devoted to elaborate ritual; the Dobus of Melanesia, whose lives by our standards seem extremely unpleasant, with cheating as one of the highest "values"; and the Kwakiutls of Vancouver Island, who had a social and economic system that seems to be a parody of our own. These three cultures, out of the many that are or have been practiced in the world, are enough to show the fantastically different ways in which human beings can live.

At first sight, any other culture but our own seems utterly crazy. Further study, with an effort of empathy, makes possible considerable understanding. Other cultures are *not* "crazy"; they just see things differently. The work of cultural anthropologists such as Miss Benedict has given us insights into other ways of doing things, completely different from our own.

This leads further to the suspicion, nay, the certainty, that we ourselves are a "culture," with our ways of doing things that at first sight would seem to anyone from another culture just as "crazy" as their habits do to us. We are "natives," we are a proper field for cultural anthropological study.

In the years since I first read *Patterns of Culture* I have continually been trying to look at our own cultural habits as if I had never seen them before. The results have been astonishing, and this book records a few of my preliminary impressions.

From time to time in my examination of, and interaction with, this strange culture now prevailing in the central part of the North American continent, I have been led to some surprising heresies, some of which are recorded here. I may remind the reader that the word "heresy" has two meanings:

HERESY, *n*. Opinion contrary to the orthodox doctrine of the Christian church, or to the accepted doctrine on any subject.

Concise Oxford Dictionary.

MORE SACRED COWS

"But nac petetin petetac, tic, torche, lorgne,
or rot kipipur kipipot put pantse malf, he was
declared an heretic."

Rabelais-Urquhart

1 : *Lines on the Map*

THE LAKE OF THE WOODS, one of the largest American lakes after the five Great Lakes, is partly in the United States and partly in Canada. From a point, approximately in its southwestern corner, the U. S.-Canadian boundary is the 49th parallel, which runs uninterruptedly to Vancouver Sound. From the southeast corner of the lake, the boundary is the Rainy River, which lies a little to the south of the 49th parallel. Thus, the southernmost part of this lake is in the United States. The remainder of the lake is mostly in the Canadian provinces of Ontario and Manitoba. But not all. On the western shore of this lake there is a projection, a sort of rounded cape, or not-very-sharp promontory, which is United States territory. This bit of land, some 124 square miles, less than one twenty-thousandth of the land area of the United States, is connected by land to Canada, but is unreachable from any other part of the United States except with an airplane or a boat.

This came about through a historical accident. Shortly after the American Revolution, when boundaries had to be decided on even in extremely remote western territories, it was agreed that the Rainy River was to be the boundary up to the Lake of the Woods. The Treaty of Paris, 1783, laid down that *U. S. territory was to extend to the most northwest point of the Lake of the Woods*. This is an agreement that has never been abandoned or even questioned, during a number of further treaties, agreements and protocols, throughout the nineteenth century, and a number of surveys to determine, and mark, where the "most northwest point" actually is. The fact that the decision was inconvenient never entered into the various discussions; the only problem considered was how to draw the international boundary westwards from the Lake of the Woods. In general, the boundary in the region to the west was to be the 49th parallel, which was the northern boundary of Louisiana as ceded by France in 1803. But the inconvenient, though unquestioned, "most northwest point" lies to the north of the 49th parallel. In 1842 it was agreed that the boundary should run southwards from the northwest angle to the 49th parallel, even though that left an "enclave" of U. S. territory within Canada. Further surveys and agreements ensued, and the latest adjustment was made in 1925, whereby the "most northwest point" was moved nearly a mile south to avoid having the deep-water channel of a certain inlet cross the international boundary no less than five times.

Northern Minnesota, in general, is not thickly populated, and its geographical curiosity, the northwest angle, has no settlements of any size. It would be perfectly simple to hand it over to Canada. It would be necessary to change (or revise, or repeal, or revoke, whatever the diplomats might call it) the Treaty of Paris. A treaty is a man-made thing, and there is no question that it can be changed by men, whenever there is any plausible reason for doing so. In 1783, the intention was to run the boundary from the northwest point due *west* which would have avoided any enclaves until the Mississippi River was reached. But it was found later that such a line would never intersect the Mississippi at all, for the river does not go that far north. And so some sort of join had to be found between that point and the 49th parallel, inconvenient as it was. And in all the subsequent surveys and discussions and agreements, throughout the nineteenth century and up to the entirely minor adjustment of 1925, that "most northwest point of the Lake of the Woods" was held as a fixed, utterly unshakable point of law, as if it had been engraved on stone by the good God himself on the top of Mount Sinai.

To turn now from northern Minnesota to a more southerly clime, in the balmy Caribbean is a pleasant archipelago, the Virgin Islands. It lies about forty miles to the east of Puerto Rico, and consists of seven main islands, St. Thomas, St. John and St. Croix, area 135 square miles, pop. 31,000, and Tortola, Virgin Gorda, Anegada and Jost Van Dyke, area 59 square miles, pop. 7,600. They are mentioned in two groups because the first three belong to the United States, the other four to Great Britain. Yet they are culturally and economically very closely related, and in any sensible way of doing things would be considered as one unit. From Tortola to St. John at the nearest point is about one mile. But an arbitrary line divides them.

History, of course, is at the back of this, and the silly situation only persists because of history. The U. S. Virgin Islands were formerly Danish. The Danes settled St. Thomas and St. John in the seventeenth century, and later they bought St. Croix from France for 750,000 French *livres*. The other four islands were settled by Britishers from way back, and they have been colonies of Great Britain for some three hundred years.

United States interest in the Virgin Islands goes back nearly one hundred years. During the Civil War, they had been a convenient neutral port for Confederate shipping. Secretary of State Seward, who had concluded the purchase of Alaska from Russia for $7.2 million, negotiated with the Danes for the purchase of St. Thomas and St. John for $7.5 million. The sugar trade was profitable at that time, and it would be convenient to have a domestic source of sugar. A plebiscite was taken of the voting population of those two islands, who declared themselves 98% in favor of the change. The contract was formally concluded by the highest representatives of both governments in 1867, and was ratified by the Danish upper house, the Landsthing. But the U. S. Senate refused to ratify the treaty and the deal fell through.

After the Spanish-American war, when we had acquired Puerto Rico, and an interoceanic canal figured large in our plans, there was renewed interest in the purchase of the Danish Virgin Islands. The sugar trade was no longer so profitable as it had been, and we were able to negotiate for the purchase of all three main islands (plus associated smaller islands) for $5 million. The inhabitants were less enthusiastic than in the first flush of enthusiasm after the Civil War and the liberation of the slaves—after all, they had heard of lynchings in the United States—and no plebiscite was taken. The Senate ratified the treaty, but this time the Danish Landsthing did not.

At the time of World War I, an intense preoccupation of

the U. S. Government was the safety of the Panama Canal. During that war, it seemed entirely possible that the Germans might win, and they might then overrun Denmark (they did not do so during that war, as they did in World War II). What would happen to the Danish Virgin Islands if this took place? There appeared to be a very distinct possibility that these Caribbean islands might fall into unfriendly hands. The islands were then on the verge of economic ruin, but such was the concern in this country about a remotely possible menace to the Canal that the Danes were able to sell them to us for the sum of $25 million. We have been pouring money into them ever since.

The present situation of the U. S. Virgin Islands is a peculiar one. They resemble New York City in just this one respect, that they have a Puerto Rican problem, for Puerto Ricans, of course, are allowed free immigration into this other part of the U. S. dominions, and they are somewhat resented. British subjects from Tortola and the other B. V. I. frequently go over to the U. S. V. I. to work, and the economies of the two groups are so closely connected that the U. S. dollar, rather than the British Caribbean dollar, is the regular medium of exchange in the B. V. I.

Both groups of islands are liabilities, rather than assets, to the countries that "own" them. The British find that they have to do proportionately more for them than they do for their other West Indian islands, owing to stimulation and competition from the U. S. V. I., and since everything has to be done with the U. S. dollar, it costs them at a higher rate. The inconsistencies of U. S. laws have caused hardship to the islanders, such as the McCarran act of 1952, which created legal difficulties in the usually routine passage of "immigrants" from the British to the U. S. islands. So also do the abominably logical consistencies. In 1939, and again in 1953, cattle shipments from the B. to the U. S. V. I. were stopped on account of cattle tick fever. This was under a regulation intended to prevent the import of infected cattle from the *Mexican* border, but being a U. S. law, it was made applicable to *all* U. S. territories, whether it made sense under local conditions or not. And in the V. I. it made no sense, because the cattle in all these islands are equally infected, irrespective of the man-made division. And the situation is also inconvenient to the United States because the close proximity of "foreign" territory affords a round-about but effective route for illegal immigration.

The British Virgin Islands are the only group of British islands that decided not to enter the Federation of the British West Indies when it was formed in 1958. They continue to be Crown colonies, administered from Whitehall, but with all their economic and social life closely connected with the United States. And can anything be done about it? No.

It is easy for us to blame Her Britannic Majesty, or rather Her Majesty's Colonial Office, for what we in this country may tend to think of as a somewhat intransigent attitude in regard to these islands. But are we any better, when it comes to our own border with Canada? Let us suppose that the suggestion were seriously made, in a practical way and on a political level, that we regularize the boundary by handing over the northwest angle to Canada. One can imagine the shouting and orating and arm waving and table banging and the stormy weather on Capitol Hill that would be generated by the Senator from Minnesota! "What! Give up one square inch of the sacred soil of the sovereign State of Minnesota—" It would be as if there were a proposal to make a public slaughter of a sacred cow. *Any* Senator from Minnesota, whatever his true private opinion (if it is not a contradiction in terms to speak of the "true" and "private" opinions of a politician), would be bound to do this, for it would be political suicide not to.

It is worth noting that, on the rare occasions when an international transaction of this kind takes place, as in the purchase of the Danish Virgin Islands, it is *not* real estate that is transferred. All landowners who held real estate in the Virgin Islands under Danish law continued to hold the same real estate after the transfer. Anyone who owns property in the Northwest Angle would, if it were transferred, continue to hold his property, only he would pay such taxes as are levied in Canada, instead of the State of Minnesota. When real estate changes hands, it is customary for the new owner to pay him who relinquishes the property, since real estate is invariably an asset—only on the rarest of occasions, presumably, is it a liability. But when *sovereignty* is transferred, who is to pay whom? In practice, of course, the government taking over the new sovereignty always pays something, as in the U. S. purchases of the Louisiana territory, Alaska, and the Virgin Islands. But this is because such a transaction is never made unless the purchasing country has some very strong reason for wishing to take over the territory. In general, and apart from special strategic considerations, sovereignty is not necessarily an asset. The Federal Government and the fifty states do not hold the territory over which they have their respective kinds of sovereignty as a producing investment, in the manner of a man who has a small savings account or a solid block of United States

Steel. The government discharges its obligations to its citizens, and it collects money from them with which to do this. If it loses a few square miles of territory, there are fewer citizens to collect taxes from, and fewer citizens to do things for. What's the difference? The incoming and the outgoing of money, to and from the government, are balanced over the country as a whole; they are not necessarily balanced for each little piece of territory. It may be that some areas contribute more than their fair share of taxes, whereas others are on the hand-out end of government money to a greater extent than on the cough-up end. It could well be that, on the balance, there are some territories which we should *pay* to give away. Yet do we ever do it? No. Even to suggest such a thing would be a heresy— "contrary to the accepted doctrine."

We cannot see our own *mores*. We can only see the peculiar behavior, that is to say the *mores*, of those distant from us. Ruth Benedict, Margaret Mead and their fellow anthropologists go to strange, usually rather primitive countries and add to our stock of scientific information their findings on the habits of the "indigenous personnel" (to use the Army's carefully chosen unloaded phrase). It would be interesting if some of these "personnel" could come here and do the same for us. But it would be too difficult. They have not sufficient sophistication and we have too much sophistication, too much complication, for anyone to treat of our love life like *Coming of Age in Samoa*. All that comes out is Kinsey. Our social life and our economic life are far too complicated for anyone to understand. Certainly we do not understand them ourselves. No banker, no economist, really understands our money. For accumulated, piled-up irrationalities, what could exceed our political life? Except perhaps this—our fetish-like worship of man-made lines drawn on a map.

Our state lines are just as bad as our international boundaries. Apart from entirely minor adjustments it is utterly impossible, in the realm of practical politics, to change them. Yet the boundaries of the states are not conveniently drawn. A number of our largest cities each lie tucked away in a corner of a state, whereof the state capital, very plausibly chosen so as to be nearly central, is quite an unimportant town. In many cases, rivers were chosen as the state boundaries, which seems plausible when virgin country is being settled, but becomes less and less convenient as the country develops, because cities tend to grow up on *both* sides of rivers, and thus they become divided by state lines. In this way, Missouri has the greater part, but not all, of two cities, Kansas City and St. Louis, at opposite ends of the state. For New Jersey the breaks have been the other way, for it has the grubby suburbs of New York City and of Philadelphia, but no large city of its own. But can anything be done about all this? Politics, or rather *mores*, utterly forbid.

If a Martian astronomer were studying the earth through a powerful telescope, he would not see it as we are accustomed to think of it. We cannot (as yet) look at the earth from a sufficient distance to see more than a minute portion of it at one time, and to get a Martian's eye view we must use the eye of the imagination. But when we do this, we think not of the earth, but of the map. And the map shows the whole land surface of the earth divided by arbitrary lines into areas which are commonly colored differently in order to strengthen us in the illusion that these man-made lines represent realities.

The Sahara Desert is crossed by curious diagonal lines marking the limits of the various French administrative divisions. Not that there is much to administer in the middle of the Sahara. South of the Sahara, on the coast, where the land has always produced valuable colonial products, the map resembles a punched card ready to be put into one of those intelligent sorting machines, with the little niches where the various European "powers" were able to grab some valuable part. Now these artificially delineated territories are, one by one, rapidly gaining their independence, and becoming self-governing territories in their own right, with their own color on the map, not the borrowed color usual for the territories of this or that colonial power. In the former French and Belgian territories the Western language spoken by educated nationals is French; in the former British territories it is English. The English-speaking territories use pounds, ounces, gallons (Imperial), inches, feet, yards and miles. The others use the far simpler metric system. The Russian and Chinese Communist worlds, which stand ready to leap into Africa with all the avidity and even more rapidity than the nineteenth-century European powers, use the metric system, which gives them a great advantage.

In the former Belgian Congo they might, perhaps, re-arrange as they please the lines that divided the provinces, but they could not obliterate the "international" boundary that separates Congo (Leopoldville) from Congo (Brazzaville) to the north, even though both countries speak the same language, French. Still less could they ignore one of those lines drawn some time ago by Europeans and take in the Kingdom of the Kongo, which lies directly to the south and west of them in northern Angola. And yet these lines that seem so irrevocable are nothing else but what the boundaries were for the original colonies. They do not correspond in the least to cultural or ethnic realities in Africa, but reflect the greater or less successful rapacity of European conquerors, as modified by subsequent political deals.

Not only Africa, of course, but the whole land surface of the globe is crisscrossed with these peculiar lines, which to us are so important, but which the Martian would be unable to see. In every continent there are places where the lines are arbitrary, inconvenient and even absurd, but it seems to be beyond the power of us mortals to change them. To take only one example out of ever so many, the small West Indian island of St. Martin is divided right down the middle by a line which makes the island half-French and half-Dutch. A twenty-foot-thick wall of concrete, one hundred feet high, if it had to be moved, would present a simple problem. An arbitrary line on the map, man-made and therefore, one would think, removable by man, is so difficult to change that no one ever takes it up as a challenge.

The separate areas on the map, each colored homogeneously with one color, are of very different size. Canada, the United States, Brazil and Australia are all of the order of three million square miles. The area marked "U.S.S.R." is very much larger than this. Other such areas are smaller, much smaller, and very much smaller still down to Andorra, Liechtenstein, and a few other such oddities. In a few cases one country consists of two geographically separated bits. Pakistan consists of two blobs, East Pakistan and West Pakistan, which are about a thousand miles apart. Between the two World Wars, Germany was in two noncontiguous parts, divided by the Polish Corridor. Another example of this kind of oddity is the United States of America.

It is taken for granted in our civilization that every single square inch, not only of the habitable world, but of the entire land surface of the globe, whether habitable or not, *must* be allocated to one or another of these sovereign nationalities, and colored appropriately on the map. No gray areas are allowed, all is some brilliant color: red (rather inappropriately) for the old British Empire, other colors for other sovereignties as the map maker's fancy takes him. Every person alive in the world must have some nationality, which is inscribed in his "papers" (one cannot live without papers in the modern world), and every spot on the earth that is not covered at high tide, every barren island, unreachable mountaintop or uninhabitable desert must "belong" to some country or other.

Egypt is a country which has recently achieved its own color on the map, whereas it was formerly painted over with sloping pink and white stripes to indicate the loose sovereignty of England over its territory. Now there is in the neighborhood of Egypt a tract of land, very dry and inhospitable, which happens to have immense importance to the whole world because it is the site of the Suez Canal. By the rules, it has to belong to some country, and since it would make no sense to give it to Israel, it had to be given to Egypt. It is *not* part of Egypt in any genuine sense, in any manner of speaking that is in touch with realities rather than manmade fictions. In such a sense, Egypt is the extremely fertile delta of the Nile and a long narrow strip of the Nile valley. This has been Egypt for millennia. But in the lines-on-the-map sense, it has been ruled, in entirely recent times, that Egypt "is" a large hunk of territory, extending from the Red Sea to some hundreds of miles west of the Nile, most of which is useless, unprofitable desert. And in the map-making sense, the expression "Egypt" was held to include the territory surrounding the Suez Canal and the Sinai peninsula, simply because there was nothing else that could be done with this territory.

After Nasser had nationalized the Suez Canal, in 1956, he became involved in armed conflict with Israel and with interventionary forces from England and France. In spite of the fact that his incompetent army was thoroughly trounced by the Israelis, he has been playing up this action, ever since, as a resounding victory. He has been using all his resources of propaganda to get the Egyptians to react "properly" to this insult, this outrage, this bare-faced, brazen attack upon *Egyptian* territory, this violation of the borders of a sovereign state. Egyptian postage stamps (the only form of propaganda that is exported to any extent) show a harmless, likable, peaceable Egyptian family, father, mother and kids, being terrorized by bombs dropped from foreign planes, bombs dropped upon *their* territory, their *own* country, their *Egypt!* It suited his purpose to encourage the inhabitants of the Nile valley and delta to think of every square inch that is enclosed by those man-made lines as their own sacred motherland (or is it fatherland in Arabic?) and to react to any violation of these borders with an unappeasable sense of affront. If a single square inch of the map area of Egypt were "violated," every Egyptian was to react as an Englishman or American would if Buckingham Palace or the White House were destroyed by a foreign bomb—or if a tiny Caribbean island or part of the shore of a northern lake were to be changed on the map. How well Nasser is imitating our Western *mores!*

Nasser is undertaking an extremely difficult, and necessary, task. He has a population of twenty-three million (rapidly increasing) who are existing at the lowest level of standard of living. They have to pull themselves up by their own bootstraps (if indeed they wear boots). This will be a task of gigantic magnitude, and no ordinary, quiet, jog-along methods will do it. The Russians stand ready to undertake the job at any time—in their own way. Nasser may receive help from the Russians, but he seems to know that he cannot expect the Russians to do the job for him; if they were to do it, it would scarcely be *for him.* He is compelled to use drastic measures, and if he can succeed, it will be greatly to his credit if he can do it without the Communists' ruthlessness and disregard of human rights. Neither can he do it alone; he must have the enthusiastic co-operation of all the twenty-three million Egyptians. But for many centuries Egyptians have not been notable for enthusiasm. And so one of his first tasks is a psychological one, to get the poverty-stricken fellaheen to believe in themselves, to believe in the future, to believe (incidentally) in Nasser, to have some feeling for *their* country, and some determination to get up and get going and make it a better country than it has been in the past. He must instill into his countrymen some of our Western feeling of national pride. In so doing, he takes our "national pride" feeling at its silliest, along with its desirable features.

Similar considerations, perhaps, may animate de Gaulle with his hysterical insistence on "la gloire." His country has fallen into a slump (not through increasing but through diminishing population). In order to pull themselves out, Frenchmen will have to work hard. But as a slogan, "work hard" is devoid of appeal. Probably the only effective appeal for Frenchmen is to the great past glories of their country. It was not economically necessary for France to explode an atomic bomb. On the contrary, in strict terms of francs and centimes it is probably a luxury they can ill afford. It is true it was "only" an old-fashioned atomic bomb of the kind that obliterated Hiroshima and Nagasaki (perhaps improved), and it produced only a small amount of fall-out by modern standards. It could not, of course, be exploded in the middle of France, but the Sahara desert was conveniently available, painted all over (on the map) the same color as France to show that it was theirs to do what they liked with. But the middle of the Sahara, although uninhabited, is surrounded by inhabited countries, who were not consulted about the proposed explosion and were naturally perturbed about radioactive debris on their doorsteps, and have remained indignant ever since. And just at the time when Russia, the U.S.A. and England had managed to come to an uncomfortable agreement banning (or postponing) nuclear tests, it was peculiarly irritating to everyone on this planet for one more country to get into the act.

After thus crying "we too" to the atomic club, the French also had to join the space club. Early in 1961 they rocketed a rat ninety-one miles above the surface of the earth, and recovered it alive in the nose cone. A space rat is at any rate harmless, for it generates no radioactive dust, but it is extremely expensive, and France has better things to do with that much money. But de Gaulle presumably felt that "la gloire," which formerly demanded only fireworks, can now be served by nothing but atomic fission or an ICBM. Perhaps he has this faint justification, that to wake out of torpor the inheritors of the glory of Wagram, Austerlitz, the Marne and Verdun, nothing else would make a loud enough bang.

But what of that Martian we spoke of before, eyeing us through his telescope? We may try to imagine him, unsatisfied with his distant view of our planet, coming to visit us in his space ship. We must imagine him to be rational, and highly intelligent, or he would not have been able to invent a space ship. Let him come to this earth, learn to communicate with us in our various languages, find out what we do, and learn from us, by asking us questions, our reasons for doing what we do. It would be a tremendous intellectual task, but if he were endowed with immense perspicacity, he might eventually learn to see this planet, not with the eye of the telescope, but as we see it, covered all over with irrational lines.

Within each area delimited by lines lives a group of people, usually speaking the same language, and usually sharing some cultural and historical traditions. The Martian would soon find that nothing on this planet can be understood without history. However much he ascertained of the state of affairs right now, our present behavior would never become comprehensible to him until he had informed himself of past events, not only one and two generations ago, but hundreds and even thousands of years ago. He would learn that some of these lines separate nations who hate each other (the French and the Germans, and many other examples), but that others, such as the U.S.-Canadian border, separate peoples whose manner of living is all but identical, and who never get into more than trifling frictional situations. In ever so many places, all over this planet, he would notice the crazy peculiarities of our mad patchwork of lines, and would wonder why we do not do something about it.

He might wonder, for example, why Gibraltar is not part of Spain. If he were capable of great empathy with us earth beings, he might be brought to have some inkling of the strong feelings that Englishmen have about Gibraltar. But if he spoke impartially to everyone, and did not favor Britishers, he would also discover the subdued resentment with which Spaniards regard that anomalous situation at the southern extremity of their country. To regularize that particular boundary situation, and to return Gibraltar to Spain, would be an intense blow to the pride of all Englishmen, and if the Martian were capable of understanding pride, he would be able to sympathize. Perhaps he would be able to understand it better if one of our psychologists were to describe it to him in terms of "ego involvement."

But what sort of "ego involvement" do we have in the northernmost corner of the State of Minnesota? Not the slightest. And are there perhaps Englishmen, or West Indians, who have intense sentimental feelings about the British Virgin Islands—may they never become un-British, whatever it may cost in the way of local inconvenience? The Minnesota boundary at any rate causes no particular hardship. It is just an absurd situation that ought to have been remedied long, long ago, as soon as the unexpected situation with regard to the Mississippi River and the 49th parallel was discovered. But the simultaneous and closely contiguous existence of the B.V.I. and the U.S.V.I. is not only an absurdity, but an inconvenience and a hardship. It could be remedied by a stroke of the pen. It would have to be the pen of a V.I.P.—of several such persons in fact, the President of the United States (the action ratified by the Senate) and their opposite numbers in Her Majesty's realm. But it could be done. It would take time, and an immense amount of hot air would be expended in doing it, but the deliberations and the orations and the protocol would only amount to a mass of verbal flimflamflummery, which would hurt no one. Our Martian would have a hard time in understanding why it is not done. Much as he might admire us earth dwellers, he would sadly report to his home planet that in certain areas of rational activity among us, the pen is clumsier than the sword.

2 : *We-Feeling*

"Two AMERICANS were sitting at a bar. The first American was the brother of the second American. But the second American was not the brother of the first American. How could this be? What relation was the second American to the first American?"

Answer (for those of limited imagination): "Sister."

This story, quite obviously, comes from England, and it may be mentioned that it is at least slightly funny there.

But what, indeed, *is* an American? Does the expression perhaps mean a United-Statesian, if there were such a hideous word? There ought to be such a word, for there is no one-word way of designating a citizen of the United States. A Canadian is an American and so is a Mexican; so also a Panamanian, a Peruvian and many others. In the synthetic language, Esperanto, there *is* a word for a United-Statesian, "Usonano." It is both masculine and feminine, so that it would lend itself to that silly British joke.

The situation is just as bad over there. There are definite and clear distinctions between the terms "United Kingdom," "Great Britain" and "England," but it is hardly worth explaining them to any United-Statesian. Personally, I have lived in the United States long enough to be able to say "I'm British," although the expression would have turned my stomach in the days when I lived in England. "I'm English" is what an unchanged native Englishman says. (What the Scotch and the Welsh say I do not know.)

But what *is* an American? As the word is popularly understood, he (or perhaps she) is free, *white,* and twenty-one.

Suppose I am anywhere in Europe, and I say to someone, "I would like you to meet a friend of mine, Manoel Coelho, from Brazil." No one is surprised if Senhor Coelho turns out to be the color of café-au-lait. I said he was Brazilian, didn't I?

Now suppose I say, "I want you to meet another American, I mean United-Statesian, or Usonano, Mr. Robert C. Weaver or Rev. Martin Luther King." There is a tiny tinge of surprise when these well known personages are seen. "Why didn't you tell me?" This question *may* actually be spoken, and it is there in thought, in any case. Because these people are what "an American," as usually thought of, isn't.

We-feeling is very subtle. The U.S. Virgin Islanders have a we-feeling that excludes Puerto Ricans, although it includes British Virgin Islanders. In the United States, our we-feeling does not always cover the entire population. "We" or "us," when spoken by a white American, always means "we white Americans."

Senhor Coelho's country, Brazil, is very different indeed. Although the population ranges from the fair-haired and blue-eyed (and these not always first- or even second-generation immigrants) to the darkest skins that can be found anywhere, it would be utterly impossible—even if anyone

should think of anything so monstrous—to run a Jim Crow
car on a train. There would be no dividing line anywhere.
Only a small proportion of the population could be assigned
definitely to either Jim Crow or non-Jim Crow. For all the
rest, the conductor would have no way of saying where they
belonged. When a Brazilian speaks of "we," he means "we,"
the entire nation.

In the other countries of the world, the degree of we-
feeling is extremely various. England, for example, has a
wonderfully strong we-feeling, with immense national coherence. The way the English stick together, during wars,
is unmatched anywhere else. They have done it during two
World Wars, and they are quite prepared (*if* it is humanly
possible) to do it again. Between wars, they "grouse"
("gripe" or "beef"). During wars, they grouse too, but they
have an ingenious technique of grousing loudly about the
little things so as to make the bigger troubles bearable. When
the bombs are falling—a situation which would probably
drive us Usonanoj to unbelievable panic—they dig in and
become more nationally coherent than ever before. Their armies have a reputation for being good in a *losing* situation, a
virtue which is extremely rare. Many an army has been fine
in a series of dashing victories. The invasion of continental
Europe in 1944 called for one part of the line where an expected strong counterattack was to be resisted doggedly;
General Eisenhower gave this position to British troops, and
they did not let him down.

Of course, it is a smaller country, and perhaps it is easier
for it to achieve a we-feeling than a country of the size, and
with the problems, of this one. Thus, Great Britain (often
referred to in this country as "England") took into itself,

and into its we-feeling, both the Scots, who formerly spoke a different language, and the Welsh, who still do. There are crackpot independence movements both in Scotland and in Wales, but they are the lunatic fringe. A Scotsman-Englishman national quarrel usually ends with both parties with their arms round each other's shoulders, and with beer mugs raised high for gigantic toasts, each to the other's country. An exchange of national rivalry between a United-Statesian and an Englishman is never like that. There is always a note, or at least a tiny undercurrent, of bitterness and envy on the part of the Englishman.

The English have traditionally been beautifully free from color feeling, as long as they stayed at home. The reason for this is that the indigenous population of England does not contain any Negroes, or any race that is visually different. As soon as they get to the colonies, those colonies where there are white settlers as well as "natives," their attitude changes markedly. In the Republic of South Africa, where there are plenty of Englishmen, they behave like South Africans. They carry this behavior over into Kenya. Even in Australia, there are enough natives to make the white Australian decidedly color conscious. The New Zealanders, however, are decidedly better. In England itself, they are now beginning to have problems. Their laws permit West Indians to come to England, and not only as visiting cricket teams (which have long been highly popular) but to stay in England and work. England offers more opportunities than many of the islands, and a number of very dark-skinned West Indians are now living and working in England. When the English get to the point where they realize that this creates a problem for them (and it occasionally erupts on a small scale already) they will not find any solution to it easily.

The Portuguese, in their African and other colonies, combine brutal treatment of the "natives" with a comparative absence of race feeling. The French are much the same. If a man from Senegal or Dahomey speaks beautiful Parisian, knows Corneille and Racine—and reads Sartre before breakfast—he *is* a Frenchman. He has inherited the Champs Elysées. The Spaniards are the same, or nearly so. We sometimes hear of riots in Spanish-speaking cities, such as Medellín or Rosario, Caracas or La Paz, but they are not race riots, as in Montgomery or Chicago. And yet the French and Spanish, and especially the Portuguese, are the worst colonial administrators, just as the English are the best.

But Paul Robeson, in search of a country where he would be free from animosity based on the color of his skin, chose Russia. He was quite right. The proletarian revolution is not for the benefit of any particular race, but for the whole of mankind. "The Internationale unites the human race," according to one of their revolutionary songs (which, as is usual among revolutionary songs, with the striking exception of the Marseillaise, is sung to a dismal tune). The Russians have carefully and elaborately set up a we-feeling for the oppressed and downtrodden proletariat of the world, regardless of nationality. They do not practice National Socialism. They aim for socialism without nationality.

When a Russian says "socialism," by the way, he means what we call communism. What we call socialism, which is roughly the state of affairs obtaining in Sweden, is for him just a debased form of capitalism. In the Russian vocabulary, Russia is still in the first stage after the glorious revolution and the setting up of the dictatorship of the proletariat. Fidel Castro is semantically correct, according to the Communist way of understanding words, in describing Cuba as a "socialist" country; he is semantically incorrect according to our way of understanding words, for Cuba bears no resemblance to Sweden. The Russian-Chinese-Cuban stage is called socialism, and is defined as "from each according to his ability, to each according to his work." From there on, they hope to be able to arrive at communism, which is defined as "from each according to his ability, to each according to his need," although some doubts have been expressed, by Russians themselves, as to whether human nature can ever be changed that far.

If one is talking to a Russian through an interpreter, one should always remember this difference. If the interpreter is extremely good, and if he is a Westerner, he may translate as follows: translating into Russian, "socialism" would be rendered as "state capitalism as in Sweden," and "communism" would be translated "socialism," whereas translating out of Russian, "socialism" would be translated "communism," and "communism," if the Russian used that expression, would have to be rendered as "the state of affairs they hope to arrive at, some day, in Russia." But if the interpreter were a Russian it would be useless to expect him to observe any such subtlety. It would be a wasted effort to make any attempt to explain to him that different languages really are different, that words that sound extremely similar may have quite different meanings, and that the job of an interpreter is to convey the *meaning*, whatever words may have to be used. Russian interpreters, translating out of Russian into any other language, insist upon translating "socialism" as "socialism," although this is not the word that conveys the meaning the speaker intended. As they see it, anyone who supposes that "socialism" describes Sweden, or "communism" the present state of affairs in Russia, is just misinformed and *incorrect,* and it is the duty of any Russian interpreter to put him right.

"Socialism," as conceived in Russia, is international, and never on a national basis. Even when they got into trouble with the Hungarians, this was not, in their view, because the Hungarians were nationalists, but because they were "reactionaries," which is a convenient word they have for anyone who opposes whatever the Russians want to do. True National Socialism was exemplified by Hitler and the Nazis. The expression was fully descriptive. Hitler, who had occasional touches of genius, realized, right after World War I was over, that there were then only two forces in the world capable of moving men strongly, nationalism and socialism, and he determined to harness both of them in his new movement, National Socialism. Perhaps there was not so much socialism, in any sense, but the nationalism took the form of a conscious, deliberately worked-up feeling of belonging to a master race, all other races being inferior. This was the essence of what we commonly call fascism. We use the word "fascism" presumably only because "nazism" or nazi-ism" makes an awkward word in the English language. What it refers to it not so typical of the Fascists as of the Nazis. It resulted, among the Germans, in an extremely strong we-feeling, but of an unspeakable kind. Thank goodness, or thank God, it has been defeated.

Russians are not even anti-Semitic, as anti-Semitism is understood, and either practiced or felt as a slight under-

current, in most other countries of the world. They have
no objection to Jews as people, and they feel not the slightest desire to cremate them or gas them. But they do not
like Jews to behave like Jews. In the Jewish culture or religion (whichever it is), a small proportion of the population
spend the greater part of their waking lives in reading Torah,
and in theological discussions. There are magnificent stories,
from Germany, of rabbis who walked calmly into the gas
chamber, continuing their quiet, even-tempered disputes until the last possible moment. The remainder of the population
are attentive to the Torah in varying degrees, but they all
feel themselves as belonging to the group, to the race, to
the culture, to the religion. This creates a we-feeling within
a we-feeling, which in Western countries is entirely tolerable,
but not in Russia. For it means that Jews, if they behave
like Jews, have some loyalty, some demand upon their attention, their energy and their activity, that is not the State.
The State, the proletarian revolution, the maintenance and
improvement of "socialism," and the transition to "communism" demand complete adherence of everyone. Once that is
granted, there is no trouble on account of race. In their vast
work of organizing and developing that huge part of the
world that lies between the Urals and the Pacific, the Russians have been very careful not to interfere with local languages and, as far as possible, with local customs. In
Tadjikistan, in Yakutia, among the Buriats, the Oirots and
the Uzbeks, the children are all taught their own language in
the schools, and also Russian as the scientific and technical
language, the language of advanced culture, and the universal language of the future. They are permitted, even encouraged, to keep up their national songs and dances, and

their picturesque national costumes. Thus the whole of northern Asia is, within the U.S.S.R., a sort of museum of minor
national cultures. There is even Birobidjan, an area inland
from Vladivostok, set apart for Jews. American correspond-
ents who have visited it have described it as a shabby and
neglected place.

But when the Russians set up, say, a steel plant in India,
they have an immense advantage. They all understand completely that the plant is being set up for the Indians, to be
run eventually by Indians. It is as different as can be from
a British or American oil refinery in Southern Arabia or
Venezuela. Every Russian engineer or technician, working
on such a plant, knows that his job is simply to train his
opposite number, an Indian, to do the job himself, and he
does it without condescension.

When the Egyptians "nationalized" the Suez Canal, there
were dire predictions that they would not be able to run it.
It was believed that the extreme skill of the British and
French pilots, learned by many years of apprenticeship,
could not be learned by anyone in a hurry, and in any case
never by Egyptians. But Nasser, who owes a great debt to
the British and French for providing him, by their military
action against him, with such a wonderful opportunity for
increasing the we-feeling among Egyptians, put in some
Egyptian pilots, and they have worked the canal with entire
success ever since. Furthermore, in a certain respect of public relations, they have done the job even better. For the
Egyptian pilots are reported to be unfailingly courteous,
whereas the British and French pilots were haughty to all
ship captains except those of their own select "we-feeling"
group.

It is exceedingly difficult for us white United-Statesians, or for Britishers, to talk with Asians, Africans or even South Americans, without condescension. We feel them to be not only foreign, but also inferior. Or even if we genuinely and sincerely do not have any feeling, on the conscious level, of the inferiority of Asians, Africans, etc., *they* feel it. They are terribly sensitive to any insincerity, and they are likely to cross over that fine line that distinguishes such sensitivity from the imagining of slights where none are intended. This is the result of many years of colonial domination, whose residue is not obliterated so easily.

And yet, the future of the whole world, including us, depends acutely on what happens, in the following years, in the "uncommitted" nations. The Russians are not associated with these memories of colonial domination; never having had African slaves, they are not thought of as resembling old-style plantation "massas" or Georgia crackers. This gives them an immense advantage over everyone in Western Europe and North America above the Rio Grande. The Russian rape of Hungary and the Chinese barbarity in Tibet are like two battles which the enemy has deliberately lost, but they are far from being the whole campaign. If we are to have any friends at all in the world of the future, if we are not to be bottled up in our own bit-sized slice of the North American continent, we will have to develop a color-blind we-feeling. And we cannot do this abroad until we first do it at home.

Of course, it is a standard repartee from the hard-boiled white Southerners that "nigger lovers" are "Communists." And indeed if it were a crime to have anything whatsoever in common with Communists, then anyone who wishes to see the race problem solved in this country would be a criminal. Communists *do* want to see the brotherhood of man, regardless of race, over the whole world. So do we. Communists also believe in living, breathing, eating, etc., and so does everybody else. They believe in maximizing industrial production, as who doesn't, although there are sharp differences as to how this shall be done, and how the products shall be distributed. If we were to allow that everyone who agrees with Communists in any particular were guilty of infamy, the Communists would be able to lead us about by the nose with the greatest of ease. For they could stop us from taking *any* line of action, simply by recommending that action themselves.

We have in this country, in favor of complete social equality between races, a considerable body of opinion among whites and probably complete unanimity among Negroes (except for a permanent ground swell of minor movements based on Black Supremacy). This amounts to a good many million people (the exact number does not matter, neither can it be ascertained) who agree with Communists in at least this one respect. But our methods of doing things are decidedly different. In any country that is "liberated" by the proletarian revolution, it is "love your working neighbors of all races—or else!" We propose to do things slowly, gradually, the quiet way. When we cannot get an ell, we will take an inch, and come back later for the other inches (how many inches make an ell, anyway?)

An illustration of the Communist way of doing things was provided by the famous Scottsboro case. In 1931 nine Negro boys who were riding (illegally) on a freight train, were falsely accused of raping two white girls, who were also on the train illegally. The first trial, at Scottsboro, Alabama, was a farce. The Negro boys were all sentenced to the electric chair (except one, aged 14, who received a mistrial). The International Labor Defense took up the case of this gross miscarriage of justice, and succeeded in having the death sentences stayed, and a new trial ordered, on the ground that the boys had not received proper legal defense. The I.L.D. was also very successful in arousing tremendous public interest in the Scottsboro boys, throughout the United States and indeed all over the world. In the years that followed, the moves and countermoves to get the boys released, and the successes and partial failures, make a long and complex story. The Scottsboro Defense Committee, which was most active in the case, found itself handicapped by the fact that the I.L.D. was Communist controlled.

The I.L.D. raised, throughout the world, huge sums of money (estimated to be of the order of a million dollars) "for the Scottsboro boys." The amount actually spent on the most important of their various trials was $60,000, so it is probable that vast sums went into the coffers of the Communist party. The I.L.D. organized parades everywhere, with marchers carrying banners, the slogans characteristically beginning with the words "We demand . . ." They threatened the judge, and the Governor of Alabama. They tried to make the whole thing into a class issue, describing the hatred between whites and Negroes in the South in terms of the proletarian revolution. Although their attempts to cast the white farmers and small-town people as "wicked capitalists" were ludicrous, they greatly hardened and intensified the feeling in the reactionary South that "nigger lover" and "Communist" are synonymous, and this has made things far more difficult, ever since, for anyone who tries to work for improved race relations.

The Communist press (the *Daily Worker*) declared that it would be no use to take the case to the Supreme Court. In the Communist view, all courts are organs of capitalist repression, devoted only to keeping the rich firmly in the saddle. While the Supreme Court was in session, the I.L.D. were exceptionally active with their marchers and banners. The nine justices, solemnly considering the legal arguments concerning the second trial of the Scottsboro boys, threw it out and demanded a new trial on the ground that there had been no Negroes on the jury list. The I.L.D. promptly claimed the credit, declaring that this success was due to their silly parades!

Later developments ran into other difficulties. One of these was that the most brilliant lawyer for the defense of the boys, Samuel Leibowitz, met with exceptional antagonism in the South because he was a New York Jew. And the Scottsboro Defense Committee was gradually forced to the conclusion that the I.L.D. was dragging its feet, and did *not* really want the release of the boys, for the reason that they would be of more value to the Communist party—nuisance value— in jail than out!

Eventually all the boys were either released or paroled, except one, Haywood Patterson, who escaped. After he had made his way to Detroit, in 1950 he was found by the F.B.I.—but Governor G. Mennen Williams refused to extradite him. Years later this was to have quite unexpected aftereffects. President Kennedy's appointment of Williams as Assistant Secretary of State for African Affairs was greeted with huge enthusiasm, for Williams was well known and admired all over that continent for his refusal to send Patterson back to an Alabama jail, and for his other good work in race relations in Michigan. So well had the I.L.D. done their publicity work! But to the I.L.D. the unfortunate nine boys were never human beings, suffering from a terrible injustice; they were figures, they were pawns in the greater struggle, a struggle which they saw in terms of pure good and pure evil, and complete victory, or nothing at all.

Communists do not really want to make things better, at least not inch by inch. In their theory, everything will be put right after the proletarian revolution, and so the way to solve all problems is to lead towards this revolution. But a revolution is like a boiler explosion; it demands pressure. Therefore they work towards building up steam pressure, for the explosion. Far from solving problems one by one, they deliberately try to make them worse, so that eventually all can be solved at once, in one big proletarian bang. For them the end justifies the means. They do evil that good may come. The trouble with this approach is that the good may not come, or it may come mixed with evils that are as bad as the original ones, and possibly worse.

We tackle a little bit at a time. We also tackle one problem at a time or, at least, one problem considered as isolated from others. When things have become sufficiently bad for the proletarian revolution, *all* problems are to be solved. But we are modest in this respect also. In solving the race problem we do not expect that other problems will be solved at the same time, in particular, the great permanent world-wide problems of Rich and Poor, whose polysyllabic sociological designation is "distribution of wealth." Far too many people in this great and wealthy country of ours are poor. What is to be done about it? Certainly something must be done. The Rich-and-Poor problem is tied up, in this country, with the race problem, for it needs no statistician to tell us how rare Negroes are among the very rich, or that the proportion of very poor is much higher among Negroes than it is among whites. In Marxist thinking, where everything goes by an economic interpretation, the two problems are very closely connected, and the subjection of Negroes is deemed to be one device used by the bourgoisie to insure a plentiful supply of cheap labor. In Christian thinking, although the two problems may exist in an intertwined state, they are separable in that it is possible to solve one without solving the other.

Can the Rich-and-Poor problem ever be solved? In the words of our Lord, "The poor ye have always with you," and this may be a significant prophecy. Quite apart from such considerations, if anyone comes forward with any kind of proposal which he thinks will eliminate poverty and achieve a reasonably equitable distribution of wealth, he will have a hard time showing that his proposal is feasible. For he cannot point to any society (above a very primitive level), existing either at the present time or at any time throughout history, where this problem has been solved. All through history, wherever and whenever methods of production were good enough for anything appreciably higher than bare subsistence, there were rich and poor, often very rich and extremely poor. In the world of today, outside of the Communist countries this is still the case, and inside them, there is quite a spread between the successful commissar and the modern equivalent of a moujik, the little fellow who has no special ability and does not need to be rewarded much for whatever work he is made to perform, to say nothing of those persons, reported to be comparatively numerous, who are misfits in Soviet society and are herded into labor camps.

On the other hand, anyone who would like to see a genuine, complete solution to the race problem in this country *can* point to countries where, in spite of the necessary ingredients being present, the problem did not and does not exist. In the Roman Empire, it appears that there was no such thing. If a man could not speak either Latin or Greek, he was a barbarian, but if he had either of these accomplishments, he was accepted regardless of his color. In the later Roman Empire, we often read of such and such a notable person that he was "from Africa," but such was their color-blindness that we simply do not know which car he would have ridden in, in a Jim Crow train, had he been alive today. Among modern countries, the Soviet Union can be pointed to, as Paul Robeson found. But this famous singer could just as well, as far as race relations are concerned, have gone to almost any country in South America. He would have found a notable absence of color feeling in Brazil, even though that country, like this one, has a history of settlement by Europeans, with African slaves. The slaves were liberated later than in the United States, as late as 1889, but nevertheless the color problem, as a problem, does not exist.

We propose to solve the color problem, even if this is not accompanied by a simultaneous solution of the problem of poverty. As for poverty, although we do not know that we can ever abolish it, we must never tacitly accept its existence, but do everything we can at least to alleviate it. Poverty is a terrible evil, painful, humiliating, degrading, and usually harmful to the soul, and we must never be complacent about it. We must always be working towards a partial solution of the poverty problem, at the same time that we are accomplishing the complete solution of the color problem.

We must always proceed at a steady rate of progress; we cannot afford to stand still. Steady progress in race relations means that there will be resistance. The Supreme Court decision calling for integration of public schools, and the Freedom Riders, have had the effect of considerably hardening the opposition. The die-hards in the South now try to intrench themselves even more firmly (although they know in their hearts that they are fighting a losing battle), and the moderates, who thought that they were doing well in aiming for a "separate but equal" state of affairs, are discouraged when they see this hardening of the line. This is as it should be. Absence of resistance would mean absence of progress. We cannot let the most reactionary of white Southerners dictate the pace!

There is so much that has to be explained, to white Southerners and very often to white Northerners as well. For one thing, that social equality does not mean that one cannot choose one's own friends. There is social equality among whites, but this does not mean that all whites must be my friends. Even under perfect conditions of racial equality, I would choose for my friends, among Negroes, only those who have a sufficiently similar social and educational background to my own, and who are personally sympathetic to me. In other words, I would choose them just the same as I choose any of my other friends. For Southerners, it is often difficult to imagine *any* Negroes who would thus qualify. In New York City, where I live, there are quite a number of people who have friends who are either white, or dark skinned, or anything in between. And there are also white people who are so leaning-over-backwards liberal that they go out of their way to make friends with Negroes, whether they like them or not. They are practicing color discrimination in reverse.

For white Southerners, even for "Southern liberals," who often fail lamentably to have a full grasp of the situation, there is always that one dark and dreadful question, that one unmentionable thought, that hideous midnight fear lurking in the background—race mixing! They do not like to have this brought near the surface in any conversation, for they turn green at the gills and suffer a sick feeling in the stomach. This is an extremely intense human feeling, and like all human feelings must be respected. How can it be dealt with? It is usually not helpful to throw everything all at once at an unreconstructed Southerner. But it is not right to leave the question entirely alone, unchallenged. Some answer, based on reason, love and moderation, must be given, and must be given with kindness.

"But you believe in race mixing! You want to mongrelize the race!" When this question crops up, it is at least possible to point out that the question, as phrased, is not the right question. It is based on all-or-nothing thinking. White Southerners want very desperately, for reasons that are not valid, to maintain the "purity" of the white race. But in the intensity of their feeling about this, they are incapable of seeing that a person who does not share their passionate concern by no means necessarily *wants* to bring about the exact opposite! He may be entirely indifferent in the matter.

Suppose, for a moment, that the race problem in this country were entirely solved. Everyone would make friends, with no regard to color, from their own social and economic groups. For many generations the situation would still be that white people, making friends within their own cultural group, would have mostly white friends, and the friends of Negroes would mostly be Negroes. Most marriages, for some time to come, would be between people of more or less the same color. But not all. Every so often a young couple, differing in color, would want to get married. Their parents might object—but parental objection has never stopped many marriages. And so mixing of the races would take place very slowly, extending over many generations. It would take place of its own accord, without anyone, still less with any one group, "wanting" race mixing. The only sense in which anyone "wants" race mixing is that it is a symptom, or a sign, of a satisfactory state of affairs. It is by no means desirable for its own sake, neither is it undesirable. It is just utterly indifferent.

Of course, the rules as at present set up assure the eventual triumph of the Negro anyway; that is, if one is to continue to think of distinguishable groups of people, "whites" and "Negroes," instead of just plain "us," and if one is to think of the situation as competitive so that a "gain" to one group is a "loss" to the other. The present ground rules are as follows: a person is white if *all* his ancestors (barring extremely remote ones) came from that section of the human race, in Europe, where (presumably as a result of some strange mutations far back in prehistory) pigmentation is markedly less than in the human population as a whole. But a person is regarded as a "Negro" if *any* of his ancestors came from Africa. If it were possible to maintain the population in two groups without any interbreeding whatever, then it might be feasible to keep up the present situation permanently, with neither group gaining over the other to any considerable extent. But there is always some interbreeding. There has been interbreeding in the past, so that the majority of U.S. Negroes are by no means of pure African descent. At the present day, interbreeding takes place to some slight extent even in the South, and to a much greater extent in northern cities. But by the rules, the offspring of any such mixed marriage are always regarded as Negro. *Any* percentage of mixed marriages, projected indefinitely, will eventually result in a larger and larger proportion of the population in the "mixed" group, and if these are to be counted as Negroes, the time will eventually come when there are no more "pure" whites. The remarkable thing about this entirely unsymmetrical arrangement is that it was set up by whites. The whites themselves made the rules, and they made them in such a way that they are bound to lose in the long run.

But of course there is no question of "losing." There is simply *us*, the "we" of the United States of America, and we know that all of our descendants, a number of generations from now, will be of that color which will make a Jim Crow train or a segregated drinking fountain or lunch counter impossible. But what is our attitude to this? Do we welcome it? Or regard the prospect with reluctance? It is not easy to learn our own minds about this without some deep heart searching.

Imagine the state of affairs, many generations from now. Suppose that the race problem has been solved, and that the "race mixing" which will follow upon this as an inevitable, but unimportant, consequence, has had time to proceed considerably. Think, as we did before, about two Americans sitting at a bar in Europe—"and the first American said to the second American . . ." Never mind what silly joke about Americans (United-Statesians) may be current in Europe at that time. What will the Europeans understand, or imagine, as "an American"? Certainly not what is understood now. What would a caricature of "an American" be like? One might imagine a cartoon in Krocodil (if that magazine is still going, and with the same editorial policy) showing a wicked capitalist, plotting war from his office in Wall Street, with features decidedly darker than a Muscovite's.

As of the present, when we white Americans travel in Europe among the English, French, Dutch, Germans or Scandinavians, it is almost impossible to resist having a trace of a "we-feeling" with these people on account of our all being white together. And if we admit to this feeling, how shall we welcome the inevitable future? If we look upon the future with even a tinge of regret, we are to that extent working against it.

In Manoel Coelho's country it is different. Brazil is even more of a melting pot than the United States, with Portuguese settlers, African slaves, many native Indians, and later immigrants from Poland, Germany, Italy and other countries. They have a phrase for their own future, they speak of the "raça Brasileira," or Brazilian race. This gives them a we-feeling that does not work against the future, but with it.

We too must solve the race problem. But we do not, as yet, have a positive idea in our minds of what We Americans are going to be like when the problem is solved. We must eventually get to a state of affairs in which it would not cause the least surprise to find a white person as a servant in a Negro household, or a white man as a hired hand on a Negro's farm. But until we can think of a person's social status as something entirely separate from the color of his skin, and until we think of "we" as we really are, and not as part of our population only, we still do not have the right kind of we-feeling.

3 : *The Relative Heresy*

I'll have grounds more relative than this.
—Hamlet

RELATIVITY is not a scientific heresy. It is a scientific truth.
But this truth has led, in a most indirect way, to perversion
of the meaning of a word, and unclear thinking. This is a
minor heresy. But related to it, and greatly facilitated by it
(although it is far older) is the Relative Heresy itself, which
is at least big enough to be worth bothering about.

Everybody uses the word "relative" constantly. When we
use this word, we often have some idea of what we mean by
it. When we use its opposite, "absolute," we usually have no
idea at all. Yet the word "absolute" formerly had a fine, clear,
useful meaning, and "relative" also had a meaning, although
quite different from what it is apt to mean now. Hamlet
is using the word in the older meaning; "more nearly absolute" is what a modern would say; or perhaps "less relative."

There is nothing inherently wrong in words changing their
meaning. We have many words in the English language that
have changed their meanings greatly, sometimes with amus-

ing results. "Amusing" is a nice example of such a word; another example is "nice." This results in its becoming quite hard to read anything written, say, two hundred years ago, but in nothing worse than that. Words are like tokens that stand for ideas; we pick up ideas and shuffle them around, and we communicate them to other people's minds by means of words. Sometimes a word becomes unstuck and attaches itself to another idea. No matter—provided we keep track of the switch. But if an idea gets left without any token to handle it with at all, we have lost something. If a person has "infer" and "imply" trouble, or says "like a cigarette should" instead of "as a cigarette should," only the dictionary makers and the grammarians will worry. But if he thinks that "there's nothing either good or bad, but thinking makes it so," that is the Relative Heresy, and it is important.

What does "relative" mean? An aunt is a relative. But to hear the word used in ordinary conversation, one would hardly think so. We hear that "time is relative, and space is relative, for Einstein has proved it," and although the person saying these things hardly ever has any precise idea of what he means, his vague suggestion is that there is something uncertain, something that doesn't stay put, about time. And space too—both of them seem to be subject to a sort of pleasing indefiniteness. And yet an aunt is as definite as can be. She is either an aunt, or she is not.

An aunt is a relative simply because she has a niece or a nephew, and for no other reason. She is an aunt because one or more persons have a specified *relation* to her. A true relative always expresses a relation between one thing and some other thing, and that other thing is the *correlative*. The correlative of "aunt" is "niece" or "nephew," of "father" is "son" or "daughter" (or "offspring"), of "double" is "single." It is characteristic of a relative term that it doesn't make any sense at all except with the necessary implication of its correlative. No one is an aunt all by herself; there has to be the niece or nephew. "Ancestor" necessarily implies "descendant." Nothing is "far" except in relation to something "near," nor does "high" have any meaning except in contrast to "low." A modern word, often misunderstood, which has a relative meaning is "isotope." It refers to atoms having the same atomic number as other atoms of the same element, but having different atomic weight. Nothing is an "isotope" all by itself, it has to be an isotope *of* something. Other relative terms, nearer to everyday life, are "friend," "enemy," or "lover," for not one of these words makes any sense except in relation to somebody else.

Any comparative is always relative; "better," "larger," "more expensive," "louder," or "uglier," for it is always perfectly clear that there is something to which comparison is made. Obviously, nothing can be "better" all by itself. But can a thing be "good" by itself? or "large"? "expensive"? "loud"? or "ugly"? This is where confusion begins to come in. Take "large": if there were only one thing in the universe, it wouldn't be large. It wouldn't be small either, it would just be. Merely to say "large" is to imply some sort of comparison, with something.

You may hear someone say, "You call him tall, because he's six feet one, but after all tallness is relative, just think of those basketball players, six foot seven and even more." This is true, for tallness is relative. If there were only one man (or one thing) in the universe, he wouldn't be tall. You may also hear someone say "This man [or it might be this book, or this wine, or this piece of music, or anything else] is good, but there are some that are better, and certainly there are some that are much worse, and even the very good ones aren't completely good, and the worst have some good in them. After all, it's all relative, there isn't any absolute good." This is not true, as thus expressed. For good is *not* the correlative of bad. They are related as opposites, but not as correlatives. They are related as white and black, which again are opposites, but not correlatives. "Better" is certainly a relative, for it necessarily implies something else that is "worse" or "less good." But good does not necessarily imply bad, any more than white implies black. If there were only one thing in the universe, it could be good. If a man, or a book, or a wine, or a piece of music, is good, then it *is* good, without any necessity for comparing it with any other man, book, wine or music. In this sense—and it is the only possible sense—there is an absolute good. This does not mean that you could find an "absolute good" kicking around somewhere, perhaps abandoned in someone's garbage can, or that "the absolute good" is a thing that you could see, hear, feel, smell or taste. It means only that goodness is decided without reference to badness, just as whiteness has no necessary reference to blackness, and is quite different from, say, "upness" or "beforeness." Of course it is true that different people, or different things, possess goodness to different degrees, just as also things can be gray, but it is one of the minor misunderstandings to think that for this reason "good" is "relative."

A major misunderstanding, and one that is aided and abetted, if not caused, by the theory of relativity, is to think that "good" is "relative" on account of the fact that people would not necessarily agree as to which thing is good, and which not. If different people are making a judgment of the same man, some of them might not recognize certain virtues that he had, some might give grave importance to vices that others would consider trifling, and they might even disagree as to the standards, so that some of them would consider a virtue what others would think of as a vice. This is profoundly true, and this sort of disagreement is the source of a large amount of the trouble in this world. But it does not mean that "good" is the *correlative* of "bad." Each person, when judging whether a certain man is good or bad, or rather how much of good and how much of evil he has in him, makes a judgment according to his own *absolute* standards. Petty thieving is a virtue according to gypsies, a vice according to almost everybody else; each is judging according to absolute standards—they just do not agree as to what those standards are.

"Different for different people" is the modern understanding of the word "relative." It springs entirely from the scientific theory of relativity, but it does so in a most roundabout and curious way. The theory of relativity is a marvelous triumph of human reason, and its object is precision of thought, but by a most remarkable twist it has come to generate confusion as a by-product.

A noteworthy thing about the theory of relativity has been its extreme popularity, from the very beginning. This is only partly due to the admirable and lovable qualities of Dr. Einstein himself. It is also an expression of a characteristic of our age. But we, who live right in the middle of our age, cannot see its characteristics without what appear at first to be mental gymnastics. We seize readily upon the agreeable features of African art and Zen Buddhism, but to some strikingly unbalanced features of our own culture we are utterly blind.

It is quite common for artists to paint pictures showing several views of the same thing at once. A face will be shown in full-face and also in profile; or perhaps a bridge will be shown in successive views as one passes under it. Artists will say that "Relativity has shown us that space and time are relative. And art should be contemporary, keeping in touch with the main movements of the times. Science is the most important, the most exciting development in modern life, and it gives us our inspiration for these new ways of expressing ourselves." This is of course an entirely harmless by-product of relativity, but it is admirable and remarkable that an interesting trend in art should be inspired by a scientific theory of which the artists themselves have not the faintest understanding.

Relativity, as an influence on our thinking, is in two stages. But these are not the two stages that scientists are familiar with, for Einstein developed the Special Theory of Relativity in 1905, and later the far more complicated General Theory in 1915. Of these, the General Theory is (1) quite beyond the understanding of any but extreme specialists and (2) entirely without influence on our ordinary thinking. The Special Theory leads, rather remotely, to the equivalence of mass and energy, and the well-known equation, $E = mc^2$, which underlies the development of atomic energy, good and bad. Thus it has had, at many degrees of indirection, practical consequences of the greatest importance for all of us. But otherwise, $E = mc^2$ has not influenced our thinking, since, apart from the practical applications, it is of no interest except to specialists whether matter and energy are equivalent or not. The two stages that are important for the effect they have had on our thinking, and therefore on our acting, are (1) Newtonian relativity and (2) Einsteinian relativity.

Newtonian relativity is very easy. It is what often passes for an explanation of Einsteinian relativity, on an extremely low level. The term is to some extent a misnomer, almost a contradiction in terms, because it was never formulated, as such, in the time of Newton. It is a modern reading of what was implicit in the Newtonian set-up of matter, forces, gravitation and so on.

Newtonian relativity simply reveals that motion is a relative concept, a genuine relative with a correlative. It is explained by the familiar example of sitting in a train and seeing, not the platform, but another train on an adjacent track. Often one can be quite uncertain as to whether one's own train is moving forwards or the other train is moving in the opposite direction. To decide this, you have to look down and see the station platform. But are the platform and the railroad track really stationary? They are part of the earth, which is rotating on its axis and also whirling through space around the sun at a speed of nearly nineteen miles per second. And so, taking the sun as stationary, the earth is moving, and very rapidly. But is the sun stationary? With reference to our own galaxy, astronomers can show that the sun has a definite motion, which they have been able to specify and measure approximately. And what about our galaxy? Is it in motion? Merely to ask the question is to see that it can only be answered by reference to some other galaxy or assemblage of galaxies. Motion is in all cases decided with reference to something else. If there were only *one* thing in the universe, it couldn't be said to be in motion; the idea would be entirely meaningless. And this is one test of a true relative.

The other test of a relative is to find the correlative, and in the case of motion there is a slight subtlety. For the correlative of "moving" is not "stationary" since nothing can truly be said to be stationary, not the earth or the sun or even our galaxy or any group of galaxies. To find the correlative, we have to specify the motion a little more precisely. Was your train moving, say, eastwards, or was the other train moving westwards? Is your elevator moving upwards, relative to the building, or do you choose to regard (as you can if you wish) the elevator as stationary and the whole earth with building attached to it as moving downward relative to the elevator? Motion is always relative to something, and it is always motion in a certain direction, the correlative being motion in the *opposite* direction. This is all there is to Newtonian relativity—a simple subject.

Now there is one thing that characterizes this particular relative, motion, and distinguishes it from all the other relatives. It introduces the idea of *different for different people.* If *we* are in one train and *they* are in the other, we may think that we are "stationary" (as if that word had any absolute meaning) and that their train is moving, while they may say, "Oh no, it is *you* who are moving." What we can agree on is that there is relative motion between our two trains. We may disagree when we ask the question "Which train is the moving one?" and we find that the answer to this question is one thing for us, another for them, so that it is "relative" in the modern meaning of the word.

The Einsteinian theory of relativity goes far beyond this.

It considers not only "motion," but "space" and "time" themselves, and comes to remarkable and unexpected conclusions about them. Briefly, the conclusion is that space and time are not "absolute," as was thought previously, but "relative," where the meaning of "relative" is nothing else but "different for different people." This was the conclusion that came like a bombshell to the scientific world in the early years of this century, and was accepted avidly. There was some opposition to it, but not very much, although of course there was plenty of discussion of it, until its ideas became understood and comparatively familiar to those scientists who were concerned with it. The theory was popularized, and extremely successfully, right from the very beginning. One of the best popular accounts, by the way, was written by Dr. Einstein himself. By the 1920's the phrase "time and space are relative" had become a commonplace, and it has remained so until today. It is actually understood by some physicists, but by no means all. It is misunderstood, to a greater or less extent, by numerous physicists, by very many chemists, and by a majority (or maybe all) of the biologists, psychologists, sociologists, and any others that there may be in the "behavioral sciences." Except for specialized physicists, the degree of comprehension of relativity has been practically nil.

Like Newtonian relativity, the Einsteinian variety can be thought of by starting with people in trains or, rather, with "systems of observers," as they should be called with full formality. These systems of observers are moving, relative to one another, at very high velocities, much faster than trains, for the effects of Einsteinian relativity do not become appreciable except at fantastically high velocities, approaching that of light. Our own "system of observers," by the way, includes anyone who is not moving relative to us; he may be close to us, or very far away, but as long as he moves along with us (if we do move) and keeps the same distance from us, he is in our "system." The other fellow too, who is flashing past us at a great speed, has space filled with "his" observers, who are stationary relative to him, whereas we consider that all of his observers are flashing past us at the same immense velocity. We will think that they are moving, and they will think that our observers are all moving—but this is straightforward Newtonian relativity, and there is nothing in that to bother anyone.

The trouble comes in when we and the other "system of observers" make measurements, as physicists do, and start comparing them. We, and any observer in our system, can make any measurements we like, on the position and movement of the stars, the sun and the planets, the manned rockets, the unmanned exploratory satellites, the ICBM's—and all of us will be able to agree about these measurements. But it will not be the same if we try to communicate our results to the other system of observers. According to Einsteinian relativity, we and the other observers will not be able to agree on any measurements, on anything at all.

It is particularly puzzling that we will not only disagree about the lengths of things and the distances between them; we will also have fundamental disagreements about time. We provided our whole team of observers (who are widely scattered about space) with very accurate stop watches, and we had all the stop watches carefully synchronized. But we will complain that the stop watches of the other set of observers were incorrectly synchronized. On the other hand, the other observers will make the same complaint about us. They will claim that their synchronization was extremely carefully carried out and that *our* stop watches, although accurate in the sense that they don't "gain" or "lose" on each other, nevertheless give unreliable readings because we failed to synchronize them properly. And so it goes with every kind of measurement; in our system we will get this answer, in the other system they will get that, and we will never agree on any measurement.

This strange state of affairs has to do with the very fundamental nature, in the world we live in, of light and also of ultraviolet, infrared, commercial radio frequencies (both AM and FM), microwaves, radar, and a lot more, all of which together are various forms of "electromagnetic radiation." How were we supposed to be "communicating" with those other observers whom we thought of as flashing past us at a very great speed? This would most suitably be done by radio frequencies, or else by radar, or perhaps even visible light signals. No matter which, they would all be forms of electromagnetic radiation, and this is by far the quickest way of transmitting a signal from one point to another. Light travels at 186,000 miles per second. But this is not only the fastest speed for a *signal* from one point to another. It is also a limit on the speed at which *anything* could possibly move. There is a deep connection between matter and electromagnetic radiation. Matter is composed of atoms; each atom has a positively charged center surrounded by negatively charged electrons; when matter is in motion, the movement of these electrical charges constitutes an electric current. An electric current generates an electromagnetic field round itself; these currents and electromagnetic fields then interact, generating electromagnetic waves, which are precisely the things we are communicating with—and without carrying the train of thought any further it can be seen that there is room for surprising consequences when we consider, in precise detail, what happens if we attempt to communicate between two *moving* systems.

Einstein's theory (the Special Theory, that is, not the General Theory) considers these matters, and provides a scientific solution of the curious problems they pose. It is based upon, and has been confirmed by, scientific experiments which bear only a remote resemblance to these "systems of observers." It is not necessary to have actual human beings moving past one another at a great rate; experiments on light rays, on moving electrons, and on various other things provide all the data necessary. The Special Theory provides some mathematical equations, and rather simple ones, for harmonizing "our" measurements with those of that other set of observers with whom we had such difficulties. The equations will harmonize the measurements of any and all systems of observers, no matter how fast or slow they may be moving and in what direction. When this is done, it turns out that nobody is "right" in the sense that anyone who disagrees with him is "wrong." It also turns out that time has this character: that the measurement of a given time interval is not the same for all observers; some will measure it longer and some will measure it shorter, according to how they are moving. Space, too, has the same character; a given space interval—say, the length of a certain object—will be measured differently by different observers, without any of them being either "right" or "wrong." Indeed, since the different measurements can all be harmonized by those mathematical equations, *all* of them can be considered to be "right."

Now it is important to note that all this refers only to the *measurement of time*, not to time itself. This is a distinction which the ordinary physicist is not able to see. For him "time" and "the measurement of time" are the same thing. "Length" and "the measurement of length" are similarly confused by the physicist, and so for everything else. If you ask a physicist, "What is length?" he will tell you how to measure the length of anything you please, that is, he will answer as if you had asked him "What is *the* length of such and such an object?" but he will not tell you what length *is*. If you ask him, "What is time?" he will similarly confuse your question with one about the measurement of time. Certain scientists, notably the great Einstein himself, have thought most intensely about the measurement of time. About the question, "What *is* time?" they have not thought at all. The most profound thinking about *this* question in the whole history of Western thought (with the possible exception of the French philosopher, Bergson) was done by St. Augustine of Hippo, and very few scientists are aware of what he had to say on this subject.

These two "systems of observers," moving past one another at a great speed, *measure* time differently. But this is not to say that time *is* different for them. Time is the same for both of them. It is, for both of them, like a continuous flow in which there is no reversal. It *is*—think about time as much as you like (it is extremely difficult to do this), but anything you can say about time (other than measurement) that goes for one system, goes for the other system also.

There is one curious by-product of this difference in measurement of time that might have relevance, not only to refined measurements, but to actual situations. This is the famous "twin" problem. One of two twins, at the age of twenty, takes a space journey to an extremely distant star (17.32 light years away) using a space ship of a kind now available only in science fiction. We may suppose that he travels at a speed of 161,000 miles per second and that he keeps this up for a number of years. Immediately upon reaching a certain extremely distant star, he turns the ship around and comes back again at the same velocity. On his return, he might find his earth-bound brother to be sixty years old, having lived through forty of our earth years; but for the traveling brother, years would be different, and he would feel, and actually be, only forty years old! His physiological processes would appear to have been "slowed down" when compared to earth time. Not only physiological processes, but *all* processes. His clock would have "slowed down" just the same as his rhythm of sleeping and eating. This would happen whatever the nature of the clock. He could have taken any number of clocks, all working on different principles, an ordinary spring-wind affair, a "radium clock" (one that measures time by the natural decay of a radioactive element), or a variety of other scientific clocks, and they would all have agreed with one another, and with his life processes. Thus the brother, while traveling, would not notice anything at all. Clocks would all be running normally, and time, for him, would be exactly the same as it is for anybody else. Only on his final return to earth would he find that all of his clocks would disagree with his brother's, and to the same extent.

The "twin experiment" has not been performed in reality,

of course, with actual traveling men; it may be that it will be tested in the laboratory by extremely precise measurements of energetic particles, if it can be arranged that a particle travels a certain distance at an extremely high rate and then travels back again to the place it came from. (Experiments bearing some resemblance to this have been performed, with results in accordance with Einstein, but the crucial feature of having the particle return to its starting point has not been done.) But the conclusion does not rest upon *direct* experimental confirmation of this kind; it is a conclusion from the theory of relativity which is so well substantiated, in so many different ways, that it hardly allows for what the lawyers would call "reasonable doubt."

In this "thought experiment" about space travel, it is necessary for the moving brother to have an extremely high velocity, comparable with that of light, and to keep it up for a considerable time, and therefore to go an immense distance; otherwise the age difference between him and his brother would amount to maybe a few seconds in many years, which would not be perceptible physiologically. Occasionally this question of "living slow" by space travel gets into the papers. When this happens, the newsmen go at once to the scientists they think will know about it, those who are working on manned rockets and flights to the moon. The answers that they receive are apt to be entirely uninformed. Space travel has not yet achieved velocities anywhere near great enough for these time effects to become appreciable in human terms. Rocket scientists and engineers do not have to know anything about relativity, which will only become an important problem for them when their rockets are vastly more advanced than they are now. Atomic physicists, and some other physicists and specialized mathematicians, are the ones who know about time differences in moving objects. They have a proposal (which they may be carrying out right now) to place an extremely accurate clock inside a satellite and have it broadcast its readings to us when it is in orbit. The practical rocket men will put it in orbit for them, but some extremely stay-at-home scientists will interpret the results.

So time is relative, then, in *some* sense. But in what sense? Something seems to have happened to the old-fashioned meaning of "relative," which required a "correlative." For if time is relative, what on earth can it be relative to? Where is the correlative? It is not even concealed beneath a semantic trap, as it is with motion, where to find the correlative we simply have to specify the motion more precisely: motion to the east is relative to motion to the west; motion up has the correlative motion down. But what can we do with time? We cannot specify different kinds of time like this. Time *always* goes forwards, never backwards or even sideways. Even for the traveling twin, time went forwards, just as it did for his stay-at-home brother. It was just that his physiological processes went slower. The Newtonian relativity of motion preserved the character of a genuine relative by having a correlative. But when we say, with Einstein, that space and time are "relative"—the *only* meaning intended by the word is different-for-different-people. My aunt!

The popularity of the theory of relativity, since the early years of this century, has been astounding. It was felt to be a great release from "the absolute," which was thought of as a little sinister in its implications. There was something exciting about being told that "space is no longer absolute."

Airplanes were being developed—man had conquered the air. Maybe this new relativity meant that man might transcend his previous space limitations altogether and visit other planets. We now know that man may indeed do this—but it has nothing to do with relativity. And as for the relativity of time, since no one could understand it, this had the fascination of mystery. It's fun to know; it's more fun to be fooled.

As soon as time and space became relative, everything else had to be relative too. And since relative was held to mean "different for different people," one effect of this new climate of opinion showed in a field which might, at first sight, seem extremely remote from discoveries in physics— cultural anthropology. For cultural anthropology is, quite literally, the study of "different people," people whose habits are widely different from ours. And if habits are "relative," so, by the new General Theory of the Relativity of Absolutely Everything, must be morals. But, whether or not it was due to Einstein, or whether it was a tendency which would have taken place anyway, cultural anthropology in this period shook itself loose from the Golden Bough. Missionaries have tried to change the habits of distant people. Frazer, who was if anything an anti-missionary, collected a tremendous knowledge of miscellaneous cultural habits, stirred them all in a pot, and then rearranged them so that they could be read somewhat like this: some of the habits and beliefs of Christians are not isolated peculiarities, but have parallels in folklore and customs from all over the world; this shows that Christianity is slightly silly.

Modern cultural anthropologists have done vastly better than Sir James Frazer. Instead of picking this bit from here and that bit from there, they have gone out to take one culture at a time and study it as a whole. In any Pacific island or remote part of Africa or South America or the hinterland of New Guinea, wherever a culture could be found more or less untouched by Western influence, they would live among the natives, living *as* the natives. This meant, of course, that they could not criticize the natives, or try to change their habits, or tell them that they were "wrong" in any way—or they would very soon have had to get out! And they did not want to change people's habits or tell them they were wrong. They wanted to *understand* them.

In studying anthropology, it is necessary to suspend, at least for the time being, any judgment as to whether the customs of a people are "right" or "wrong." In some cultures, a man must ritually eat his slain enemy; in some, a man must never talk to his mother-in-law; some cultures are polygamous, either many wives to one husband or many husbands to one wife; some cultures praise premarital chastity, others scorn it. The anthropologist, speaking or acting *as an anthropologist,* must never criticize any of these things. Any habitual conduct is right in the context of a culture in which it is considered to be right. This is known as the *relativity of morals.* And it is a heresy.

Relativity of morals has become very popular. For one thing, it permits one not to criticize, and it appeals in this way to instincts of kindness and forbearance. As the other side of the same coin, it permits one not to be criticized, and this can be very convenient. *Anything* can be justified, provided enough other people do it too.

It is one thing to practice the utmost forbearance and non-criticism with regard to a different culture, when it is practiced by a small group of people in a distant country. It becomes more difficult as the group of people becomes larger, the culture more complex, and the location nearer home. Nor is it always desirable. If I go down to the Southern states and see that Negroes are treated somewhat less than fairly there—or if I notice the same thing in New York City, where I live—am I to say, "These are the local customs, and cultural anthropology tells me that I am not to criticize"?

To do them justice, cultural anthropologists certainly would, and do, criticize this. In doing so, they must be criticizing according to *some* standard. Where did they get this standard? Certainly not from anthropology itself. Wherever this ultimate standard (not to say "absolute" standard) came from, there is a certain inconsistency. Perhaps there is something of a wavering, uncertain quality about the relativity of morals. This would not be surprising. For truth is one, and is solid; heresy, by its very nature, is scatterbrained.

What is the prevailing opinion, here and now, with regard to—any problem you like to mention, juvenile delinquency, marijuana, bubble gum, use of four-letter words in public, or bribing cops to fix a traffic ticket? Whatever public opinion says is right, *is* right. This is relativity. Now public opinion changes continually. So, therefore, does right. To believe otherwise would be to believe in some sort of absolute right— but this is contrary to public opinion (as of now, in this country).

Public opinion is made up of the opinions of individuals. "The public" is not a *thing* that you can lay your hands on, nor is it one person who can be asked his opinion on any subject, and can give a definite answer. When public opinion changes, it changes because the individual people who make up the public change their minds. In this process of change, some people have more influence than others. Newspaper editors, columnists, TV directors, and perhaps song writers have far more individual influence than "the man in the street." Good political satirists (when there are any) may have tremendous influence. But in constituting public opinion, every man's and woman's opinion is effective on the one-man-one-vote principle. *Your* opinion right now, like your vote, is required to make up the total. If you change your mind on any subject, this will be reflected in the total. And even if you do not control the editorial policies of a newspaper or a network, you do not change your mind in a vacuum. You influence others since (presumably) you talk to other people, tell them what you think, and give your reasons.

What will be the public opinion of the future? We cannot tell, but we do know with virtual certainty that it will change, in some direction. The direction in which it changes will be influenced by what *you* think and do. In which way are you going to change your mind? If you attempt to hold seriously to the principle of relativity, as at present generally misunderstood, you will have no mind of your own to change. You will merely have to wait, see what everybody else thinks, and think the same. And yet, whenever any change takes place, *someone* must initiate the change. It may be that you, yourself, initiate a change without being fully aware that you are doing it. If you do (and certainly someone does) you are discarding relativity and judging according to some principle that can only be described as absolute.

Here is one little example of how the relativity of everything works in practice. In the early 1950's the advertisers wanted to sell home permanents to little girls, for they represented an untapped market. But this was against the *mores* of our society, for girls did not start buying hair waves until high-school age. (We are told this depressing little story in *The Hidden Persuaders* by Vance Packard.) But the Madison Avenue boys were able to find a way to buck this little difficulty. They ran advertisements, in the magazines that the little girls would see, showing pre-high school girls, at parties, with dazzling beautiful hair waves. They hired psychologists to help them present "copy" that would break down the resistance of the mothers. Very soon the girls of that age group got the message and were besieging their mothers with demands for these beauty treatments. No mother likes to have to give a stern, firm *no* to what her little daughter wants so desperately, particularly when it is nothing inherently harmful, only at the most a little precocious. And mothers are not organized in a strong union, with powers of collective bargaining. And so, in any community, as soon as one indulgent mother broke down and gave her daughter one of these home permanents, all the other girls would say, "Oh *please*, Mother, so-and-so has such a lovely hair-do, all the boys looked at her at the last party." The mothers were helpless. There was nothing to do but knuckle under to the advertising men.

And yet, who *should* make the decision as to when a little girl is old enough to go all out for beautiful fixings and sex appeal? Mother should. And an incidental point is that Mother may have a hard time balancing the budget and may be making sacrifices to put by money for her daughter to go to college a few years later. It is extremely unfair that, purely for the sake of increasing the sales of this or that product, she should be in a position where it is all but impossible to avoid an extra expense for something that is not in the least necessary.

The social life of our youngsters gets more and more active at an earlier and earlier age. Perhaps as a corollary to this, so does their sex life. This is one of the tendencies of our times. But do we have to lie supine under the impact of each "tendency" as it comes along, or can we do something about it? Of course we can, provided we realize that social change is no inexorable march, driven by forces quite beyond our control. Public opinion constantly changes, and advertising men are enormously influential in this, as Vance Packard has shown us. But there is nothing sacred about public opinion (*vox populi vox Dei* is the Latin expression of the relative heresy), and we can change it *if we really want to*. In recent times we have, in this country, a most notable example of a complete reversal of public opinion. In 1919, prohibition was made the Federal law of the land by a constitutional amendment, and this is a process so hedged about with safeguards in our Constitution that it cannot be done without an overwhelming public opinion. As everyone knows, it didn't last twenty years.

A certain kind of publishing works like this. When a manuscript comes in, the publisher scans it eagerly to see whether the indecent words and the blow-by-blow accounts of sex scenes are just a little more forcible and explicit than has been the custom—and author and publisher rake in the dough. In this way the standards of publishing become continually more outrageous. And so, if our standards of permissibility in print remain those of the cultural anthropologists—"we do not criticize the manners and habits of the natives" (remembering that we are "natives" ourselves)— there is no end to it all except the gutter or the bed or the analyst's couch.

Relativity, which is the darling of our age, is a scientific theory. It has not abolished the absolute. It has abolished absolute measurements (this is true, when understood correctly, but this is not easy). Outside the field of scientific measurements—and nearly all that is of interest in human life is outside this field—we are free to adopt relativity of morals if we want to, but then we must accept all changes, wherever they go. If *you* ever object to any of the modern tendencies, if you think that anything should be reversed or channeled in some other direction, then *you* are adopting at least some kind of absolute standard. Unfortunately "absolute" is a dirty word in our culture. But it is not the sort of dirty word that induced that publisher to take that book.

4 : *Democracy in Breeding*

True, I said; and this, Oh Glaucon, like all the rest, must proceed after an orderly fashion; in a city of the blessed, licentiousness is an unholy thing which the rulers will forbid.

Yes, he said, and it ought not to be permitted.

Then clearly the next thing will be to make matrimony sacred in the highest degree, and what is most beneficial will be deemed sacred?

Exactly.

And how can marriages be made most beneficial? That is a question which I put to you, because I see in your house dogs for hunting, and of the nobler sort of birds not a few. Now, I beseech you, do tell me, have you ever attended to their pairing and breeding?

In what particulars?

Why, in the first place, although they are all of a good sort, are not some better than others?

True, Oh Socrates.

And do you breed from them all indifferently, or do you take care to breed from the best only?

From the best.

And if care was not taken in the breeding, your dogs and birds would greatly deteriorate?

Certainly.

And the same of horses and of animals in general?

Undoubtedly.

Socrates goes on to apply these principles to the well-ordered state:

> Our rulers will find a considerable dose of falsehood and deceit necessary for the good of their subjects . . . The principle has been already laid down that the best of either sex should be united with the best as often, and the inferior with the inferior as seldom, as possible; and that they should rear the offspring of the one sort of union, but not of the other, if the flock is to be maintained in first-rate condition . . . Had we better not appoint certain festivals at which we will bring together the brides and bridegrooms, and sacrifices will be offered and suitable hymeneal songs composed by our poets . . . We shall have to invent some ingenious kind of lots which the less worthy may draw on each occasion of our bringing them together, and then they will accuse their own ill-luck and not the rulers . . . The proper officers will take the offspring of the good parents to the pen or fold, and there they will deposit them with certain nurses who dwell in a separate quarter; but the offspring of the inferior, or of the better when they chance to be deformed, will be put away in some mysterious, unknown place, as they should be.

Thus Plato, in the "Republic"; in the book, that is, not in any actual republic, for he was never able to found one. And it goes for to show, not that the Greeks had a word for eugenics, because they didn't, but that they had the idea. (The *word* "eugenics," although legitimately derived from the Greek, was not used until 1883.)

Eugenics is therefore an ancient heresy. It can be called a little heresy in two senses. First, it can be called little in the sense that not many people adopt it. Breeding preferentially from "the best" has never been a wildly popular idea. It inspires a certain mild following among people who consider themselves "the best." And, secondly, it can be called little because the cure for it is exceptionally straightforward and easy. Indeed, the only interest in this not-very-important heresy lies in this, that on examining it carefully, it turns out that the remedy for it lies in the most beautifully simple application of democratic principles.

Modern interest in eugenics is, naturally, an offshoot of Darwin's discovery of evolution. Not that it had not been known, for many centuries before this, that domestic animals can be greatly improved by selective breeding, as Plato alludes to in the passage quoted. The entirely new idea contributed by evolution is that it might be possible by selective breeding of men, not only to make the human race taller or shorter or fatter or thinner as might be desired, possibly even more intelligent or more ruthless or more mild and dovelike, but to breed men into a different *species* of creature altogether. Curiously, this interesting consequence of evolution has not been widely taken up. Eugenicists—or eugenists—have contented themselves with the more modest ambition of "improving" the human race in much the same manner as has always been done for horses, dogs and cattle.

It was not Darwin himself who first brought forward modern eugenics, nor even Thomas Henry Huxley, but a somewhat less known Victorian, Francis Galton (incidentally, a cousin of Darwin). Galton was a cultivated, urbane English gentleman, with a keen intellect, an insatiable thirst for new knowledge, and a comfortable private income. In his early years he had done some notable African exploring. He is best known for his *Inquiries into Human Faculty and its Development* (1883) and *Natural Inheritance* (1889), in which he reported the results or measuring everything conceivable about human beings, inventing many of the methods of measurement himself. His minor interests are represented by the invention of a supersonic dog whistle, and measuring the boringness of lectures by counting the number of times people in the audience fidgeted.

Galton at once imagined the possibilities for mankind of his cousin's discovery, and as early as 1865, only six years after the publication of *The Origin Of Species,* he was proposing an application of the new ideas to human heredity. His work was all done before the discovery of biological inheritance through genes, and therefore is not of much value for modern science, but he was intensely interested in the possible inheritance of all qualities, both favorable and unfavorable, and devoted the rest of his life to "measuring" the extent to which this took place. Some people are more intelligent than others—is intelligence inherited? Some people are more successful than others in terms of achieving money and social status—can this ability be inherited? If so, can we not find means whereby the more successful people shall have more children than the less successful? In actual practice, Galton was quick to notice, the reverse seems to take place. On the negative side, some diseases seemed to "run in families," and were probably inherited, and it was entirely possible that feeble-mindedness, possibly even a tendency to take to drink, were inherited too. Could we not, by intelligent breeding, as opposed to the random mating that is the universal custom, accentuate the good qualities in successive generations and minimize the bad ones?

And how was this to be achieved? Towards the end of his life, in 1905, Galton became quite explicit about this. Economic advantages, enabling them to marry earlier and produce more children, were to be given to young people having the best qualities, in the form of "eugenic certificates" issued by a "suitable authority."

In the years following Galton, many people took up eugenics, as an idea, that is, not as a practical reality. It was easy to go into the slums, see the destitution, the drinking, the improvidence and the immorality, and conclude from all this that the poor represent a "bad stock." What a pity it was that a large number of ill-clad brats were always to be seen in the slums, whereas the "good stock," whose children went to Sunday School, had very few children to send there. In that period it was always easy to arrive at the conclusion that "the poor are poor through their own fault," which is a heresy, and not a little one, but a very evil and important one. Perhaps not all, but certainly some, of the eugenists fell into horrible hypocrisy. Here are some examples:

"But where strong men rise from the ranks, and then marry some weak or commonplace women of their own commonplace stock, their children soon return to the shirt sleeves of the common level. But where fortunate alliances are made with other strong strains of blood, the fortunes of the family are carried on simply because the economic, political or military genius of the family carries them on."

This is from A. E. Wiggam, who was a tireless propagandist of everything scientific and modern.* He also wrote: "Recent studies of the birth rate of college graduates by Dr. John Phillips, who has studied the graduates of Harvard and counted their children . . . certainly give us no comfort, to say the least. Phillips shows that the Harvard graduates are simply disappearing as a species of animal from the face of the earth. He shows also that the native-born Americans are disappearing with extreme rapidity, and that their places are being taken in the Harvard population by the children of foreigners who have recently landed on our shores. This is not comforting to those of us who belong to the old American stock." **

Eugenists of this period all sounded off against the weakening effects of civilization. In cave-man days the rigors of primitive life, the absence of medicine, and the dangers of combating the woolly rhinoceros and the saber-toothed tiger rapidly eliminated the genetically unfit, and kept the stock up, probably fully to the Harvard level. But civilization interferes with nature. We allow the weaker and less fit members of society to grow to maturity and even to breed. Thus, A. E. Wiggam says: "Indeed, I think it highly probable that the greatest social as well as biological disaster which civilization has worked upon man's natural constitution, especially upon his moral health, has been that it caused the man of great powers of social co-operation and rich moral emotion to take care of the man with little co-operative interest and social passion—to such an extent that the co-operative man did not have enough surplus energy left to

* *The Fruit of the Family Tree.* The Bobbs-Merrill Company, Indianapolis, 1924.
** *The Next Age of Man.* The Bobbs-Merrill Company, Indianapolis, 1927.

reproduce his generous nature in an abundant brood of children, while the non-social and the non-co-operative man was by this very process especially set up in business as a going breeding concern. It was precisely as though the glorious thoroughbreds in some famous stable were put to the plough to do the labor of the fields, while the scrubs and mongrels were kept in luxurious idleness and given the privilege of reproduction. The very softness of human sympathy and co-operativeness, which have been two of the chiefest agencies in making civilization, are also two of the chiefest agencies in breeding out the hard, robust and virile virtues. In this way gentleness keeps brutality alive, and the milk of human kindness congeals in the racial veins." *

Eugenics can be divided into *positive eugenics,* devoted to making the "stock" better, either physically or morally (though whether moral qualities are inherited is extremely questionable), and *negative eugenics,* which aims only at eliminating, or reducing the numbers of, the less fit. A number of medically defective conditions are known to be hereditary. There are deformations like harelip, cleft palate, clubfoot, or extra fingers or fused fingers, which were known to "run in families," and Huntington's chorea, a serious nervous disease which begins with involuntary twitchings of the body. Also hereditary is a tendency to give birth to mentally defective and physically deformed children of a specific type known as "Mongolian" from their supposed resemblance to Asiatics (although Asiatics think that they resemble Westerners). It was also possible, though by no means so certain, that feeble-mindedness, even just lower-

* *The Next Age of Man,* op. cit.

than-average intelligence, could be reduced by negative measures. Negative eugencis could be brought into effect by sterilization of the unfit. Sterilization, in either sex, is a relatively simple surgical operation that makes reproduction an impossibility, but in no way interferes with the enjoyment of sexual pleasure.

High hopes were entertained by enthusiasts for the efficiency of sterilization. Thus, at an International Congress for Eugenics, one speaker said, "There is no question that a sterilization law, enforced throughout the United States, would result, in less than one hundred years, in eliminating at least 90% of crime, insanity, feeble-mindedness, moronism, and abnormal sexuality, not to mention many other forms of defectiveness and degeneracy. Thus within a century, our asylums, prisons, and state hospitals would be largely emptied of their present victims of human woe and misery."

Frederick A. Rhodes, who was president of the Eugenic Section of the Pittsburgh Academy of Science and Art, and Chairman of the Pittsburgh Morals Efficiency Commission, wrote:

"There are two methods of preventing the progeny of these defectives from being a burden upon us: (1) segregation; (2) sex-mutilation [by this he means the rather simple operation of sterilization]; both of which remove their progeny from society by not permitting such children to be born. Segregation is the ideal method if sufficient suitable institutions could be provided, and the defectives detained until positively cured or past child-bearing period. Segregation is very expensive, and to detain all defectives for so long a time would be a severe burden upon the taxpayers. Segregation of all defectives even until the time of the death of each individual, although so expensive at the time, would be very cheap in the end." And he further quotes one Dr. J. Madison Taylor: "Animated by archaic notions of sentimentality, morbid softheartedness, overwrought, vitiated philanthropy and blind to teratological [*teratology*: the study of monsters] truths, there are those who insist that these derelicts shall be permitted to come freely in contact with those of the opposite sex, even encouraged to marry and beget children worse than they." *

Laws permitting voluntary sterilization were passed, and are still on the books, in a number of our states, but the actual sterilizations that have been performed permissively under these laws are not very many.

Since eugenics is directed towards encouragement of "the best" human beings, and since everyone has a tendency to think of himself, and of those like him, as being "the best," it has naturally attracted racialists. Thus eugenics becomes associated with the racial heresy, which is a very evil one indeed. When the Nazis ruled Germany they performed a large number of sterilizations. This was a gigantic and terrible heresy.

It was in the early years of this century that the work of Mendel was brought out of obscurity, and some understanding began to emerge of the mechanism of heredity, as effected by genes, carried on the chromosomes. Although the effect of this new understanding on writers on eugenics was slow in coming, much light was thrown on eugenic possibilities, particularly on the possibilities of negative eugenics. Some defects are carried by a gene which is dominant, others

* *The Next Generation.* Richard G. Badger, Boston, 1915.

by a recessive, and this makes a lot of difference. A dominant gene could be bred out, theoretically, in one generation, if all possessors of the gene were sterilized (this presupposes that all possessors of the gene could be detected). The disease would then be eliminated, except to the extent that the gene might reappear occasionally as a spontaneous mutation or as a mutation induced by radiation.

In actual practice, there would often be complicating factors. For example there is a dominant gene concerned with diabetes, but it confers no more than a tendency to contract this disease. Probably only about 10 per cent of the people who carry this gene are actually diabetic. To eliminate *this* gene would be a tedious process, going on for a number of generations. Huntington's chorea is carried by a dominant gene, but the disease usually does not manifest itself until a person is in his forties or older, and by that time he or she has usually had children, about half of whom will be carriers. Mongolian idiocy, too, is most frequent when the mother is thirty-five or older, and thus this gene often escapes detection.

Recessive genes present an entirely different picture. The quality carried by the gene cannot manifest itself except in a person who has inherited it from *both* parents. At all times there is much more in the "gene pool" than the low frequency of the disease would suggest. For example if 1 per cent of the population actually shows a characteristic carried by a recessive gene, this means that as much as 18 per cent of the population carries the gene, inherited from one parent. An example of such a recessive gene is the one that causes albinism—white hair, blue (or pink) eyes, and a very pale complexion. (It often goes with rather weak eyes, but is no more deleterious than that.) About 5 persons per 100,000 of the population are actually albinos, but 1400 out of the 100,000 carry the gene. Supposing that it were considered desirable to eliminate albinism, only the 5 albinos could be sterilized: as for the 1400 other carriers, there would be no way of finding out who they are. It has been calculated that it would take fifty-eight generations (about 1450 years) merely to reduce the incidence of albinism to one-half its present level.

In a very modest, balanced and reasonable study of eugenics, *Heredity, Race and Society,* L. C. Dunn and Theodosius Dobzhansky, professors of zoology at Columbia, state: "We have seen that the efficacy of negative eugenics programs is by no means as great as claimed by some of their overenthusiastic supporters. Only if a defect is due to a single dominant gene the presence of which in a person is easily recognizable would elimination of all the defectives lead to disappearance of the defect in the following generation, except for new mutations. But it is doubtful if any eugenic sterilization program could be so thorough in practice, and one must reckon that only a fraction of the defectives would be prevented from reproduction in every generation. Moreover, the defect might develop in only some environments, and therefore a more or less considerable proportion of the carriers of the dominant defective genes would escape being identified as such. The usefulness of the eugenics program is thereby lessened still further. Nevertheless, where dominant defective genes are involved, elimination of their carriers from parenthood would unquestionably benefit the coming generations.

"Where defects due to recessive genes are concerned, the

efficiency of sterilization is in general low. Only if a recessive defect is very common in the population can sterilization of all the afflicted persons produce a substantial decrease of their numbers in the next generation. For defects which are rare, or caused by recessive genes which show only in certain environments, or dependent on two or more recessive genes present in the same individual, very little is accomplished by sterilizing even all the defectives in a single generation. To be sure, if a sterilization program is continued for many generations, the defect will become eventually less common than it was to begin with. The process may, however, take centuries or even millennia. There is, however, a way to increase the efficacy of efforts to reduce the frequency of deleterious genes and that is to find means of detecting them in heterozygotes or carriers in whom the gene does not produce the defect. This calls for more vigorous research on the detection of carriers.

"Our opinion regarding the worthwhileness of such a program will depend on how dear to us is the comfort of remote posterity compared to the discomfort of our contemporaries. It is, perhaps, not too selfish to say that posterity should be allowed to tackle its own problems and to hope that it may have better means for doing so than we have. . . . Finally, let us not forget that treatments may and probably will be found that will relieve or cancel the manifestation of hereditary defects, as insulin relieves the manifestation of hereditary diabetes." *

On the side of positive eugenics, no one has been able to find a single dominant gene, or even a single recessive, that is responsible for any one desirable characteristic. To take

* The New American Library of World Literature, New York, 1952.

intelligence, just as an example of a characteristic that is definitely considered desirable, it is in any case greatly affected by environment, and to the extent that it is hereditary it seems to depend on such a multiplicity of genes and combinations of genes that it has completely defied genetic research. It "runs in families," certainly, but it is not confined to this. Outstanding intelligence can crop up in undistinguished families. The great mathematician Gauss is just one example that comes to mind, and everybody knows that notable stupidity is not at all uncommon in distinguished families. But it is probably true that the offspring of notably intelligent parents and forebears are slightly more likely to be intelligent than those who have not chosen their ancestors so carefully. There are many records of families that have produced men of great ability in generation after generation. In the family containing Darwin and Galton there were distinguished ancestors, and in the later generations several other able scientists and the composer Vaughan Williams. The Bach family in Germany produced not only one utterly outstanding musician but capable-to-good musicians for two hundred years. The Bernoulli family in Switzerland produced four first-rate mathematicians in two generations in the eighteenth century, and a large number of descendants, who have been carefully traced genealogically, went on, without any exceptions, to achieve success, and often distinction, either in mathematics or in some other field of intellectual endeavor. All this does not show a clear-cut inheritance of "intelligence" (whatever that may be) through one gene, but it would certainly be enough for an intelligent breeder to go to work on, if men could be bred like animals, and would make it possible eventually to develop a race of men in which the general level of intelligence and the frequency of very high intelligence would both be much higher than at present. It might not be possible to develop a race in which *everyone* would have extremely high intelligence, by present standards, but on the other hand it is questionable whether this would be desirable.

Sterilization of the unfit and encouragement, by some means of extra breeding, of the "fit" (whoever they are) would bring about a certain amount of eugenic selection, rather slowly. But positive eugenics could be speeded up enormously by the modern technique of artificial insemination. This is quite often used, at present, by couples who, for any reason, are not able to generate children in the usual way. The wife makes a visit to a hospital and is inseminated from a test tube with semen from an anonymous donor, who is often an intern in the same hospital. It is customary to arrange things so that the donor has roughly the same complexion and other obvious physical characteristics as the husband. It can easily happen that a child so conceived will elicit comments such as "spitting image of his father," and the child is in any case the biological child of the mother. Many childless couples prefer to do this rather than to adopt a child.

The eugenic possibilities of this are tremendous. It would be entirely possible for a man considered eminent in any line of endeavor to have literally thousands of children, even millions, for the number would be limited only by the number of women who would wish to have children by him. We could multiply without limit, in this way, the progeny of our most popular scientists, artists, writers, statesmen (if any), musicians, actors, singers, crooners, MC's, boxers, wrestlers, or anybody else. It would be easy for any self-styled "savior of his people" possessed of dictatorial powers to insist on being the biological parent of a whole new generation of children. Indeed, the technique can be carried further, for semen can be kept frozen for many years, and we could continue to breed biological offspring of a famous man long after he was dead. If suitable arrangements had been made, we could right now be raising innumerable descendants of Einstein or of Rudolph Valentino or of anyone else whom people might consider desirable.

These possibilities have been seized on by the modern scientific eugenists, who have at last imagined some of the possibilities for mankind inherent in Darwin's evolution. For, as they express it, "Man is now the master of his genes." Man is unique among animals in this respect that, whereas all animals undergo evolution, man *knows* that he is evoluting, and furthermore has some knowledge of the mechanism of heredity and the technical means for directing his evolution into this or that channel as he deems fit. Some scientists have elevated this into a principle which, as they see it, has at last brought to light some grand Purpose of Meaning for Life. Julian Huxley says, "There can be no action higher or more noble than raising the inherent possibilities of life," and "In the light of evolutionary biology man can now see himself as the sole agent of further evolutionary advance on this planet, and one of the few possible instruments of progress in the universe at large. He finds himself in the unexpected position of business manager for the cosmic process of evolution." Also: "I find myself inevitably driven to use the language of religion. For the fact is that all this does add up to something in the nature of a religion; perhaps one might call it Evolutionary Humanism." *

These neo-eugenists differ from the older ones—that impossibly arrogant bunch—in several respects. They have no trace of racialism, and they have escaped from the idea that the social-register, solid-bank-balance type of people represent the best "stock." Some of them have gotten very far from this; thus H. J. Muller, Nobel-prize-winning geneticist, as early as 1932 attacked the then official eugenics at a meeting of the Eugenics Society, saying, "Are the characteristics which now lead men to rise, economically, those which are the most desirable, from the social point of view? It could at least as well be maintained that the dominant classes tend to have the genetic equipment which would be least desirable in a well-ordered social system, since they have been selected chiefly on the basis of predatory, rather than truly constructive, behavior. A study of the lives of many eminent financiers confirms this. The 'respectable' captain of industry, military leader or politician, and the successful gangster are psychologically not so far apart. The high-minded, the scrupulous, the idealistic, the generous and those who are too intelligent to wish to confine their interests to their personal monetary success, these are apt to be left behind in the present-day battle." **

The modern eugenists are also, in spite of the marvelous modern techniques, much more modest in their estimate of what can be achieved by any practicable eugenic program and of how long it might take to achieve it. No more hope

---

* *Evolution in Action.* Harper and Brothers. New York, 1953.

** "The Guidance of Human Evolution" from *The Evolution of Man,* (Vol. 2., *Evolution after Darwin*), Sol Tax, editor. University of Chicago Press, Chicago, 1960.

of almost emptying our asylums, prisons and state hospitals. "Within a century we should have amassed adequate knowledge of what could be done negatively to lighten the burden on inherited deficiency of mind or body which presses so cruelly on so many individual human beings and so heavily on evolving humanity as a whole, and positively to raise the entire level of innate human possibilities and capacities"—Julian Huxley, in *New Bottles for New Wine*. One hundred years before we have the basic know-how!

This is eugenics today.

Is eugenics a heresy? The word "heresy" has two meanings, and it is possible that the answer is "Yes one way and no the other way." It is possible that eugenics is an idea "contrary to the accepted doctrine on any subject" as the Oxford Dictionary concisely puts it, if many people have a deep feeling that the thing to do is to bring up one's own children, biologically conceived in the usual manner. It is so hard to tell with people's deep feelings; sometimes they are wrong, sometimes, just as unaccountably, they may be right.

But who are "the best" people that we should breed from? This seems to be a most troublesome and thorny question. It is all very well in negative eugenics, concerned with eliminating, or at least reducing, hereditary diseases. Here, at least, we know what is desirable and what is not. Any person, man or woman, may become aware that he or she is a carrier of a truly deleterious gene. If your family has a history of hemophilia (bleeding) or Huntington's chorea or any other of those most distressing diseases that are known to be hereditary, you can consult with a human-heredity clinic, of which there are about a dozen in the United States. They are consulted widely by couples who have already had one defective child and wish to be informed about the probability, based on genetics, of any subsequent children having the same defect. The clinic may be able to advise in terms such as "the chances are at least one in ten, and possibly as high as one in four, that the next pregnancy will result in a child having such-and-such a defect," and will counsel the couple, but never tell them flat out "do so-and-so." People who find themselves in this predicament are indeed to be pitied. They may have a tremendous desire to have children of their own, and it is they who must make the decision, in the light of what the clinic has told them, whether to risk another pregnancy in the hope of having a normal child, or to use whatever methods of birth control their religion and conscience permit.

But as for positive eugenics! In this field it is hard to "accentuate the positive" for it seems to be far more elusive than the negative. This has not bothered the old-timers, of course. Plato was never a man to admit any doubt that he knew what was "the good," and the rulers were to promote good offspring by falsehood and deceit. Galton was for having the decision as to who were to be the prolific breeders made by a "suitable authority." Many of the other eugenists, even apart from the downright racial ones, always had at the back of their minds the idea that they themselves were "the best." But the modern eugenists are much less authoritarian, and though they have scarcely got to the point of recommending any truly democratic way of doing things, they are at least prepared to have eugenic selection done, to some extent, by people themselves on a do-it-yourself basis. H. J. Muller, who has come out warmly for widespread eugenics based on artificial insemination, puts it this way:

"If once it is accepted that the function of reproduction is to produce children who are as happy, healthy, and capable as possible, then it will be only natural for people to wish each new generation to represent a genetic advance, if possible, over the preceding one rather than just a holding of the line. And they will become impatient at confining themselves to old-fashioned methods if more promising ones for attaining this end are available. As the individualistic outlook regarding procreation fades, more efficacious means of working toward this goal will recommend themselves. In time, children with genetic difficulties may even come to be resentful toward parents who had not used measures calculated to give them a better heritage. Influenced in advance by this anticipation and also by the desire for community approval in general, even the less idealistic of the parental generation will tend increasingly to follow the genetic practices most likely to result in highly endowed children." *

He gives some pointers which he suggests parents should aim for in the choice of a biological inheritance for the children that they will bring up. His ultimate criterion is one that no one can disagree with, for it is the attainment of happiness:

"We need not define happiness more precisely here than as the sense of fulfillment derived from the attainment, or from approaching the attainment, of whatever is deeply desired. . . . Granted that in given cases one man's meat can be another's poison and that some find fulfillment in actually giving pain to others, most men recognize that, from a

* Muller, *op. cit.*

longer-range standpoint, these interpersonal disharmonies are undesirable, in that they allow less over-all happiness. In the same class would come a one-sided attachment to subsidiary aims—such as the satisfaction of pride in the building of pyramids or in the unlimited accumulation of luxuries—that reduces the capacity to contribute to the over-all welfare and thereby hinders the survival, expansion, and long-term happiness of the group.

"The will to self-development—hedonism, the urge to achieve—functionalism, the ideal of service—altruism, and a spiritual attitude toward existence—consecration, all these modes of approach to living, when followed up logically, become finally resolved into the pursuit of the same objective. . . .

"Surely in this society most of us could do better if, by nature as well as by training, we had less tendency to quick anger, blinding fear, strong jealousy, and self-deceiving egotism. At the same time we need a strengthening and extension of the tendencies toward kindliness, affection, and fellow feeling in general, especially toward those personally far removed from us. These impulses should become sufficiently dynamic to issue in helpful action. As regards other affective traits, there is much room for broadening and deepening our capacity to appreciate both natural and man-made constructions, to interpret with fuller empathy the expressions of others, to create ever richer combinations of our own impressions, and to communicate them to others more adequately.

"Another direction in which an advance is needed is in those traits of character that lead to independence of judg-

ment and its necessary complement, intellectual hon-
esty. . . ." *

And much more of the same.

It all sounds a trifle dull, not to say priggish.

But what do people *really* want? For if eugenic improvement is not to be done by any authority, but on an actual
democratic basis, then people would like to have children
who would grow up into the kind of people they genuinely
do want, not the kind they are told they ought to want by a
Nobel-prize winner.

I myself can certainly not say what "most people" want,
for I do not know "most people." But judging from people
I do know, and making the reasonable assumption that the
people I don't know (vastly more numerous) are not likely
to be entirely different, then, making a wild guess, I will most
boldly throw out the idea that people want two things:

1. Beauty
2. Kindness, gentleness, "sweetness" or "lovability."

They also like people to be good company—to be a good
companion, sometimes a good drinking companion. Intelligence, but not necessarily intellectuality, is often highly
thought of. To have a sense of humor is also regarded as a
desirable characteristic—or at least a sense of fun. Some go
so far as to admire a practical joker. A solid block of investments goes far to make anyone desirable, and this, too,
can be inherited, but not in a biological way. And to mention
only one other highly desirable characteristic, there is the
quality of being a good lover.

* Muller, *op. cit.*

These are of course exactly the qualities that people choose in their mates.

And so this is the way it works out—one man one vote, also one woman. What better way could there be of deciding what we should aim for in the way of positive eugenics?

The system is not perfect, of course. No one is free to pick and choose his or her mate out of the entire population. One usually must make a selection from the limited group of one's acquaintance or, rather, from those of them who are not married already. There are cases where people do not choose their mates, but have marriages arranged for them. In some periods of history this has been much more prevalent than in others; our own civilization is usually very favorable in this respect. And an inherent imperfection in the system is that people usually choose their mates while comparatively young, although their mature choice might be different. But it is not to be expected, in human affairs, that any actually existing and working arrangement will ever be perfect. We must have perfection always in front of our eyes as a goal to work towards, but we should be content (but not complacent) if we achieve no more than a reasonable approach to perfection.

Within these limits it turns out that the answer to eugenics is extremely simple—we have been doing it all along! And furthermore we have been doing it in the most beautifully democratic manner possible.

5 : *Democracy in Education?*

SUPPOSE THAT in a new country it were necessary to decide whether traffic should drive on the right-hand side or the left. If a referendum of the entire population were taken on this important matter, a majority of 51 per cent of those voting, or 50.1 per cent or even 50.01 per cent, would be quite sufficient. The decision would be binding upon everybody, and it would continue in force, unless at any later time there were a decidedly strong movement in favor of giving consideration to a change-over, for any reason.

This is not a situation that would arise often in practice. It is chosen as an example of the democratic way of doing things, not because of its resemblance to any problem that confronts us now, but because it is an extremely simple case of a problem, requiring decision, that has two distinguishing features in a very clear form: (1) it is absolutely essential that there be unanimity in following the rule, once the decision has been made, and (2) as between deciding on this, or that, there is hardly anything to be said; the *only* important consideration is to decide one way or the other, the decision to be binding on everybody.

98

Other public decisions partake of these two characteristics in varying degrees. For example, a decision to declare war on a certain country is like a rule-of-the-road decision in that it requires absolute uniformity. Once the decision is taken no citizen may dissent from it. Any one who does is treated very specially as a C.O. if he deserves this, or else he may be convicted as a draft dodger, or even shot as a traitor. But declaring war is quite unlike deciding how the traffic shall go in the second characteristic, for obviously extremely weighty considerations are to be balanced before the country is committed.

There are also matters that differ from these two in the first characteristic, the requirement of uniformity. Shall a state park or a national park be established in this locality or in that locality? We have state and national parks of different kinds, catering to different requirements. Some are in beautiful forests, some by the seashore; some contain mountains, canyons, or other natural beauties. For people do not all take their vacations in the same places. Some like sea fishing, others trout fishing; some go to the mountains, others like surf swimming. Some go to Maine, others to Florida, or to other parts and other climates within our large and varied country. And as for how public funds for vacation facilities shall be divided among these different places, there is no other consideration but the public demand. If twice as many people go to the mountains as to the sea-shore, let there be twice as many mountain facilities. And if our habits were to change, more people going to the beaches and fewer to the mountains, we could change the allocations accordingly. It is very easy to arrive at a democratic solution for *this* sort of problem, for there is not the slightest reason why any sort of uniformity should be imposed on people.

There are extremes, and all possible intergrades, in respect of both (1) and (2), the uniformity requirement, and the weightiness of the subject matter. Democracy is not always 51 per cent of the votes. Changing the United States Constitution has wisely been made very difficult indeed. It can be done by several routes, but all are time consuming and require heavy majorities, so that unless the change is favored by a very considerable body of opinion, enduring over some time, it cannot be made. In a matter which to most people was not of the greatest importance it would not be wise, in a democracy, for even a considerable majority to override a minority, if that minority happened to hold extremely strong opinions on the subject. And in some few cases, such as public-recreation facilities, there is no need for 50 per cent or more of anything; 40 per cent mountains, 30 per cent sea beaches, 30 per cent "other" would be entirely satisfactory, provided those figures corresponded not too inaccurately to the percentage wishes in the population.

How does education stand with respect to these two characteristics? In importance it is quite at one extreme, for in any country, democratic or not, it would be hard to find any issue more important than the education of the citizens. How is it with regard to uniformity? Is it one of those things in which the most rigid uniformity is mandatory, or is it at the other extreme, with the utmost variety permissible? Probably all would agree that it is somewhere in between. But where in between? This question raises the most difficult, the most dreadful problems. For it is not a simple question. It is not even an innocent question. Indeed it is a knotty, even naughty question, in fact a thoroughly dirty question.

It would be a simple question if—but it is a tremendous *if*—a very substantial majority of the population, say 95 per cent or, preferably, 99 per cent all wanted the same kind of education for their children. And it would be an innocent question if, again *if*, it were a matter of not much concern what kind of education our children were to have. It would even have some elements of simplicity if concern for education were on an individual basis, each pair of parents for their own children. But it is not simple in that way. We are all of us concerned, not only with the education of our own children, if we have any, but also at least to some extent with *all* the nation's children. For everybody's children will be the citizens of tomorrow and will form and mold the State.

The difficulty comes in with the Catholic parochial schools. These schools educate some four-million children of grade-school and high-school age (figures given here are as of 1958 since in that year a most detailed census of all schools was made by the National Council of the Churches of Christ). Although the parochial school buildings are tax exempt, they receive no other state or federal funds except, in some states only, bus rides, maybe a little milk for lunch, and a contribution towards schoolbooks. As regards all other expenses they are supported entirely by the Catholics themselves, who also pay taxes for the support of the regular schools. The Catholics, therefore, carry a slight chip on their shoulders because they pay for education twice over. Whenever there is a proposal to spend quantities of federal money in aid to education, they squawk, but on the whole they are remarkably quiet about it.

There is a special feature of *this* particular problem, distinguishing it from many others that beset us, of equal or greater urgency and importance. It is a problem that is almost impossible to discuss. Any attempt to discuss it, even to find out, among disagreeing persons, what are the principles which animate each and lead them to their divergent conclusions, generates a large amount of heat with no light. It leads to what is called an "emotional" situation, with no profitable dialectic, no meeting of minds, not even any clear exposition of divergent principles and agreement to disagree.

Now an emotional situation arises, certainly very often and perhaps always, when people's conclusions do not follow from what they say are their principles—when they do not understand their own principles. If a man is defending an attitude which he holds strongly, and if he has a deep-down suspicion that his principles are indefensible or that they do not truly lead to the conclusions he draws from them, there is nothing he can do except become "emotional." For example, if one were so unwise as to attempt an argument with a totally unreconstructed Southerner on the race question, the situation would soon become thick with emotion. The Southerner's implied principle, which he would probably not state explicitly, would have to be something like "the Negro race is inherently inferior to the white race" and his conclusion, "the races must be kept separate, with the Negroes in a state of subjection." The contrast between the weakness of his principle and the strength of his adherence to his conclusion would lead to the "emotion."

What then are the principles with regard to the spending of public money in education?

In our *mores* they are, or at least appear to be, extremely simple. It is taken for granted that the existing situation flows from, and is fully justified by, one important principle laid down by the Constitution and reaffirmed by an overwhelming consensus and by innumerable court decisions and precedents—the separation of Church and State.

"Congress shall make no law respecting an establishment of religion, or prohibiting the free exercise thereof"—Bill of Rights, First Amendment. It may be noted that this only prohibits *Congress* from making a law respecting the establishment of religion. This was because at that time several of the states still had established religions. The same idea is expressed more fully in the Virginia Act for Establishing Religious Freedom, in wording believed to be largely by Jefferson: "Be it enacted by the General Assembly, that no man shall be compelled to frequent or support any religious worship, place or ministry whatsoever, nor shall be enforced, restrained, molested, or burthened in his body or goods, nor shall otherwise suffer on account of his religious opinions or beliefs; but that all men shall be free to profess, and by argument to maintain, their opinions in matters of religion, and that the same shall in no wise diminish, enlarge, or affect their civil capacities." Equally Jeffersonian is the well-known phrase "Wall of Separation," which is first used in a letter he wrote on January 1, 1802, to the Danbury (Conn.) Baptist Association, although this phrase does not occur in any law, constitution or amendment.

If a priest, minister or rabbi were on the public payroll, would that violate the principle of separation of Church and

State? It is to be understood that he is on the public payroll for being a priest, minister or rabbi. The answer to this is "not always," for there are plenty of chaplains in the armed forces. This does not violate the Constitution, for there are chaplains of all three kinds, and so no religion is favored over any other.

What if a priest were paid for being a teacher? A large number of teachers in our public-school system accept other jobs as well. They would not (at present pay scales) be able to live and bring up their families if they did not. It is to be understood that this priest (minister or rabbi) is to be paid out of public funds *only* for being a teacher, teaching a secular subject; as soon as he stops teaching he is off the public payroll. Would this violate the principle?

In our general understanding the answer is: Yes, it would. Particularly if the question is raised concerning a teacher who might also be a Roman Catholic priest or a nun; somewhat less energetically for a minister or a rabbi or an elder of the Mormon Church. And so no priest, minister or rabbi is ever allowed to do any teaching in a publicly supported school, and public education is entirely secular.

The American Way of Life has changed considerably in the less-than-two-hundred years that we have been a republic. In the days of the Founding Fathers, all education was conducted by the various churches, and there would seem to be nothing in the Constitution or Bill of Rights objecting to this state of affairs. The idea that education is a responsibility of the State does not seem to be clearly present in writings of the period, though it may have been entertained by some. The establishment of the system of free public schools, open to all, came only in the second quarter of the nineteenth century. Later in the century the extensive system of Catholic parochial schools was set up, and has been a subject for discussion, often acrimonious discussion, and split-hair legal decisions, often split-court decisions, ever since.

In 1925 a state law in Oregon *required* all children between eight and sixteen years of age to attend public schools. This was, of course, immediately objected to by Catholics. The Supreme Court declared the law unconstitutional. Under this interpretation, the State makes provision for public education and requires that all children attend some form of school, but may not require all children to attend the state public schools.

In 1930 the Supreme Court upheld a state law of Louisiana that provided free textbooks for children in private schools; in 1947 the Everson decision similarly upheld a law in New Jersey permitting the application of tax money to bus transport for children to private schools. The private schools in question were in both cases predominantly Catholic parochial schools. These were only two instances in a continuing round of skirmishes concerning what might be called "fringe benefits." The idea of Catholics' obtaining even fringe benefits was considered, by some people, so heinous that it led to the formation of Protestants and Other Americans United for Separation of Church and State, abbreviated to P.O.A.U. This is, as might be expected, a bitterly anti-Catholic organization.

In Champaign, Illinois, Mrs. Vashti McCollum, a convinced atheist, complained that religious classes were being given in the public school that her little boy attended. These classes were a joint undertaking of some fifty local churches and synagogues, and entirely at their expense; no public funds were involved. Students were not admitted to them except at the written request of their parents, and the students who did not go to these classes were given something else to do. *But*—the classes were held inside the school buildings, and Mrs. McCollum objected to this, complaining that they gave her child a "left out" feeling of not belonging to any group.

She took the case all the way to the Supreme Court, which gave an eight-to-one decision in her favor (Justice Reed dissenting). In consequence of this decision in 1948 a public school is not allowed to give any form of religious instruction or information or to perform any kind of religious exercise, regardless of the wishes of the parents. There may be no question of any kind of democratic procedure, no taking it up with the local PTA, and nothing resembling any polling of the parents. In the matter of religious instruction or no religious instruction in a public school, the Noes have it over the Ayes whether they are a majority or a very slender minority. In fact they have it even when there aren't any of them at all!

The McCollum decision led, of course, to rejoicing by P.O.A.U., but in other quarters was greeted with distress and even consternation. Even on a legal plane, the decision was deplored by the Attorney General, Tom Clark, and editorially by the *Journal of the American Bar Association*. Many Protestant church groups were also dismayed. For there were many public schools, in many parts of the country, that were by no means so aseptically non-religious as the Supreme Court now demanded. Often there was a little daily Bible reading. In some states this was compulsory. A period of uncertainty and confusion followed, which was clarified in 1952 by the Zorach decision, relating to New York City, which stated that religious instruction to public-school pupils would be permitted on "released time," but must be *off the premises,* like the liquor license of a bottled liquor store. The State is declared to be entirely 100 per cent secular, and must not only not employ a priest, minister or rabbi, but must not allow these to give as much as a weekly half-hour pep-talk, without having the children transported to some separate, non-tax-supported edifice.

Such is the law at present. The Founding Fathers were determined to prevent the occurrence in the new country of the state of affairs at that time (and still) prevailing in England, where there is a national established church. This certainly means that the State must not favor any one particular church. Does it mean that the State can deal with the various churches, provided it treats them all equally? Or does it mean that the State must, as it were, shut its eyes and pretend that no such things as churches, or various religions followed by different groups of people, exist at all? It is the Supreme Court that interprets our Constitution, and in these recent decisions it has adopted an extreme interpretation of the ideas of the Founding Fathers, in wording of which the following is an example (Justice Black in the Everson decision, 1947): "The 'Establishment of Religion' clause of the First Amendment means at least this: Neither a state nor the Federal Government can set up a church. Neither can pass laws which aid one religion, aid all religions, or prefer one religion over another. . . . No tax in any amount, large or small, can be levied to support any religious activities or institutions, whatever they may be called, or whatever form they may adopt to teach or practice religion." (As if the activity of "practicing religion" were something slightly improper.)

And so there the matter stays at present, and President Kennedy is entirely right, legalistically, in the attitude he has taken. But it is possible at least to discuss Supreme Court decisions. It is legal for a person even to question their wisdom. It is not beyond possibility that Supreme Court interpretations may change. Indeed there has been a notable example of such a change within recent years. In the field of race relations and the equality of all men, a field dealt with in the Constitution, the Bill of Rights, and various other Amendments, the Supreme Court interpreted in 1896 (Plessy vs. Ferguson) that "separate but equal" facilities for Negroes would be in compliance with the Constitution. Nearly sixty years later, in the light of experience with the "separate but equal" theory, the Supreme Court reconsidered the matter, and in the Brown decision, 1954, ending segregation in public schools, has in effect declared that "separate but equal" will not do and that complete social integration, in schools and presumably in other public facilities, is the only principle in accord with the Constitution.

And so it is at least permissible, and it may even be profitable, to discuss whether it was wise for the Supreme Court to take the extreme position that it has taken, an interpretation that excludes not only "aid one religion" and "prefer one religion over another" but also "aid all religions." For the present position assures two things: (1) it puts the State, or at least the states, firmly in the position of being the provider of free education, open to everybody's children, and (2) it specifies that such education shall be rigidly and uniformly secular, so that any group that might happen to want a religious education for their children (not merely religious "instruction" on released time, which is a different matter) must set up their own schools, pay for them themselves, and at the same time be taxed to provide a non-religious education for other people's children!

Does the State educate? And in a democratic country, does the State educate democratically? Presumably yes, but then what *is* democratic education? Democracy in breeding turned out to be extremely simple. Can we apply the same principles to democracy in education? Or is the meaning of "democracy in education" that *every* child shall receive exactly the same kind of education? Is democracy identical with uniformity? In some matters, yes. We have seen two examples; the rule of the road is a trivial one, the matter of going to war an extremely important one, but they both have the character that uniformity is essential. Does education have this character? Should the State provide only one kind of education? If so, should it forbid any other kind of education? Or may it permit education of a different character, provided that those who want it pay for it themselves? Or could the State be regarded as the trustee of the people, whose responsibility is to provide for them the sort of education that they want for their children? Should the State be entrusted with education at all? Or is the State so much to be feared that its participation in education is, at best, a necessary evil?

These are some of the questions that must be discussed and explored and followed down to basic principles if there is to be any clear dialectic on the matter of education. And these are the principles that are obscure to people, so that they embrace conclusions passionately without knowing what principles they flow from, so that they enunciate principles from which their conclusions do not flow, so that friction and heat are generated, rather than understanding, in any attempt to discuss the troublesome matter of Catholic parochial schools.

As if there were not all these difficulties, there is yet another one which is peculiar to this country. We all fear the State, as free men should. We are most reluctant to give the State more power than the minimum necessary. Not only in education, but in all matters, it is a question of the greatest importance, and also of the greatest difficulty, how much power can be allowed to the State without diminishing the freedom of free men. And yet, in *this* country, all discussion of this is practically stultified, from the beginning, by confusion between "the State" and "the fifty states." We fear the State, as free men should, but in practice all we fear is the Federal Government. In borderline cases, where there is danger of the State's becoming too powerful, our simple but specious solution is "let the states do it." For the separate states are so much less powerful than the Federal Government that we fear them less, and we think that we can dispose of difficult questions in that way.

Concurrently, and as a corollary to the weakness of the fifty states, we also have another principle, or rather a recommendation of practice: "If you want a job done well, on the governmental level, get the Federal Government to do it." Law enforcement is traditionally the province of the states alone, but for particularly heinous crimes we have to enact federal laws. Lynching is in any case obviously a crime, but it may be necessary to make it a federal as well as a state crime. Kidnaping is so vile a crime that we have a federal law against it—provided it is done across a state line. And there is a similar law whose curious name is the Mann act, although its subject is woman. The general prosperity of the country, and the relations between labor and management, clearly cannot be dealt with on the fifty-states level, and are a federal responsibility. So also is control of narcotics. And if we are to have medical insurance for the aged, we want this to be done well, and so we want it done by the Federal Government.

We operate, then, with these two conflicting principles, because we are not clear what are, in general, the responsibilities of "the State" and what are not. We can hardly discuss the responsibilities of "the State" because of our semantic confusion between "the State" considered in general, and either the Federal Government or the fifty states. Indeed the expression "the State" taken in a general meaning is very seldom used in this country. It is familiar in only one phrase, "separation of Church and State." To speak of "the State" in any other context is to invite confusion, and it is necessary to do considerable bushwhacking through this undergrowth before we can discuss, with any clarity, what is the extent of the responsibilities of "the State" in regard to education.

"The powers not delegated to the United States by the Constitution, nor prohibited by it to the States, are reserved to the States respectively, or to the people." So runs a well-known but obscure passage in the Constitution. The states were thought of as being closer to "the people." Closest of all to the people would be local government, on the town-meeting level; most distant would be the Federal Government. A citizen was thought of as being intensely interested in his own local affairs. He would also be interested, and somewhat well informed, in the affairs of his own state. But as for that distant place, Washington (or wherever the future federal capital was to be), and questions of foreign policy—it is as if the Founding Fathers were thinking in terms of a sort of inverse square law of political interest, something analogous to the law of gravitation. Since they were educated men, fully alive to the scientific thinking of their day, it is quite possible that they did have such an idea. It would be out of the question to elect the President *directly;* each state would elect an elector, and the electoral college would haggle and take ballot after ballot—just as happens now not in the electoral college but in the party conventions. A state governor was elected directly, and he would then *appoint* the senators to Washington. But as the Founding Fathers always gave with one hand what they took away with another, a House of Representatives was set up, elected directly on a basis of rather small territorial districts.

It has all worked out rather differently. It has worked out well, on the whole, but in our day political interest does not decrease as distance increases. There is always a greater turn-out of voters in a presidential year than in a non-presidential year, which shows that the Federal Government is truly elected by the people and is very close to them. But it represents *all* of the people, over the entire geographical area, and cannot represent regional interests. Our system of government is also extremely close to the people on the town-meeting level. The intermediate level, the fifty states, represent a sort of no-man's land of political interest, not important enough for the intense interest of a presidential election, and not small enough for the intense personal participation of a purely local election.

There is nothing about the fifty states that makes them "close to the people" and therefore a particularly suitable governmental unit for education. The question is rather whether "the State," taken in any size of unit, is an appropriate organ for education. To keep the government out of business is a passion with us. To keep the government out of education is a passion too, provided the Federal Government is meant. We have recently been driven to accept the principle that the Federal Government must supply money (of which it has so much) for education. But we feel that this money must only be an *aid* to education; the actual educating, according to our *mores,* must be done by an organization at no higher level than the fifty states. But that there is the same reason for keeping the *state* government out of education does not occur to us. The Federal Government is too large to be entrusted with education. So also is a state too large. But the states manage to achieve a considerable amount of decentralization in education, giving a lot of power to local school boards. The Federal Government is not set up for decentralization. Also, it seems that the Federal Government finds it all but impossible to do anything without requiring loyalty oaths from citizens whose loyalty ought to be taken for granted unless and until they do something to call it into question. And so we have education carried out by the states, by default, as it were, simply because we have not thought of any other way to organize it, and in spite of the fact that the fifty states are not what we would choose to do any job well. Perhaps that is why our public education is so bad. For it *is* part of our *mores* that the Federal Government can levy taxes up to the limit, but a state cannot tax sufficiently to pay for decent education.

But does "the State" educate? This question refers to "the State" at any level, whether federal or state. Or does "the State" simply set up means whereby *parents* educate, by means of teachers of their own choosing?

That "the State" educates is more dangerous doctrine than might be supposed. For it is the invariable practice in totalitarian countries of every kind. It is essential under such a regime for the State to take full charge of education, to provide suitable indoctrination for the children, and to prevent them from receiving any effective counter-indoctrination from their parents. This is one of the characteristics (certainly not the only one) that sharply distinguish a totalitarian from a free country. One of the important freedoms is that parents should be free to say what kind of education they want for their own children—what kind of education, and therefore what kind of indoctrination, for there is *no* education without indoctrination.

On the other hand, the State must have considerable say in education by way, as it were, of a veto power. What language shall be used in the schools? In some countries (Brazil, Argentina) there have at times been large districts where foreign-language immigrant groups had set up schools in their own language and it was necessary to require that the national language be the main language of instruction. The State can certainly require that all schools instill a feeling of loyalty to the State. We could not tolerate schools that inculcated subversion. Neither could we permit schools to advocate, say, polygamy, communism, or race discrimination. We are already using this veto power of "the State" to eliminate race discrimination in the schools.

It is somewhere between these wide limits that the State

operates in education. We pay our tax money, all of us whatever religious persuasion, and the State provides the public
schools with it. And these schools, following the Supreme
Court decisions, have to provide an education which is entirely devoid of any religious background. Not only is it not
permissible to say the Lord's Prayer in a public school—and
quite rightly since there may be Jewish children—it is not
permissible to say *any* prayer or sing a hymn or even make
a little gesture of thanks to the Lord—on account of Mrs.
McCollum. And this state of affairs is unsatisfactory to the
parents of not only 4,000,000 Catholic children but also of
366,000 Protestant and Jewish children, so unsatisfactory
that they have gone to the trouble and expense of founding
and maintaining their own schools, in addition to paying
taxes for the secular schools.

And as if all this federal-state confusion were not enough,
there is at least one more extremely prevalent confusion in
this distressing subject. Very many people in this country
detest Roman Catholicism, and they most sharply oppose any
aid to parochial schools on the ground that they do not want
"their" money to be used to support Catholicism. Mr. Glenn
L. Archer, executive director of P.O.A.U., is naturally a
spokesman for this opinion. In a statement, November 22,
1955 (replying to an earlier statement signed by fourteen
Catholic bishops), he said: "The right of parochial or private
schools to exist is not in question. The bishops themselves
point to the phenomenal growth which their school system
has enjoyed under Church-State separation. But what the
bishops are really asserting is not the 'right' of their schools
to exist, but their alleged 'right' to exist at public expense.
This, of course, is not a 'right' but a great wrong, according

to the principle enunciated by Thomas Jefferson long ago—
that 'to compel a man to furnish contributions of money for
the propagation of opinions which he disbelieves, is sinful
and tyrannical.' "

Now let us suppose—just suppose—that Catholics *and
other denominations* had their own state-supported schools.
Never mind the feasibility of it, let us come to that later, but
just for the sake of examining principles, let us try to make
this wild assumption. It is to be clearly understood that none
of these church schools is ever to get the least bit more out of
the public coffers than corresponds to it *pro rata*—if anything
rather less. That is to say, if the Catholics in any region number 30 per cent, or 20 per cent, of the population, then they
are to get no more than 30 per cent, or 20 per cent, of the
funds available for education, and if the Seventh Day Adventists amount to 5 per cent, then 5 per cent or less is the
amount that their schools will get. The secularists are the
only group that will ever receive more than corresponds to
them *pro rata*. They are to be the sacred cows. Is it possible
to see a "great wrong" in this? Every taxpayer pays for the
support of opinions that he believes in. Not a single person
is compelled "to furnish contributions of money for the propagation of opinions which he disbelieves." Once that is
grasped, Mr. Archer's case collapses like a house of cards,
and a considerable hunk of our unwritten folklore with it.

Of course when a person "furnishes contributions" in the
form of tax money, that money does not carry a label on it
stating the religious or other opinions of the taxpayer. It is
paid into the public coffers, where all money is indistinguish-
able. He can no longer refer to it as "his" money; it is public
money, belonging to the government, the state government

or the Federal Government or the city or the township or other governmental unit. But it is in what happens to the money after it is paid into the treasury, the manner in which it is disbursed, that there is one of the most striking differences between a tyranny and a government of free men. For without question it is a distinguishing mark of a tyranny that public money is spent irresponsibly, without any responsibility to the people from whom the money has been taxed, whereas in our form of government the money is spent *for* the people, who exercise at least an indirect control over it through their election of the legislature and of key posts in the executive. In some cases, as we have seen, such as traffic regulations, where uniformity is essential, all the necessary money must be spent in some *one* way. In utterly non-controversial matters, such as the provision of public parks, there is not the slightest difficulty in apportioning expenditures to the varied tastes of the public. Nor is it a serious matter that there are some people who do not use the parks at all. The rich have their estates and country clubs and do not need public parks. But the rich are taxed for the benefit of the poor—and quite rightly too. In all cases there is democratic control of the public expenditure, and wherever appropriate there is at least an attempt to satisfy everyone in a democratic way. But in education, although the demand is for various different styles, all we are able to put forward is a most unsatisfactory compromise.

Normally a compromise satisfies at least the middle-of-the-roaders. If public opinion is extended all the way from A, at one extreme, to B at the other, the usual device for reaching agreement is to settle for something neither pure A nor pure B, but located on the scale in such a way as to be acceptable

to some 60 per cent or more in the middle, leaving approximately equal fringes of discontent at either end. Our practice in education differs markedly from this. The Vashti
McCollums, who alone receive out of public funds precisely
the education they desire for their children, are a not very numerous group entirely at one extreme of opinion. One may
suspect that there is something rather curious about an interpretation of the Constitution, however wholeheartedly
adopted and intensely held, that leads to widespread acceptance of an arrangement so devoid of any elements of moderation.

The utter frigidity of the only kind of education that the
state is permitted to provide is made tolerable by "released
time." Tolerable, but not desirable. Once a week, the children are divided up into groups, the Catholic group, one (or
more) Protestant groups, and the Jewish group, and these
groups are separately bundled into buses (if available) or
into parents' cars (again, if available) to be taken for religious instruction to proper, non-tax-supported premises.
There is always a group of children whose parents have not
expressed a desire for religious instruction. These children
cannot be allowed to go home, for then they would have
fewer hours of total instruction than the religious children;
and besides, if they were allowed to go, there would be a
dreadful drop in morale among those children who must put
up with one more bus ride and one more study period. And
so something must be done with them. But they cannot be
given any instruction that is really worth while, for then the
released-time children would be missing something! It is
necessary to dream up some occupation for them that will

keep them in school but will bear the same relation to education as non-fattening soft drinks do to food.

Many a pastor, many and many a time, has preached to his congregation that religion is not just a thing for Sundays only. Anything that they believe to be true, and any obligation that they say they will assume, on Sundays, is also for the other six days of the week. That religion is an all-the-time thing, not just a bit of hymn singing and sermon listening once a week, but a set of beliefs, and a determined, persistent attitude arising out of them, is a difficult thing for all of us adults. Even though we realize that our principles are difficult to live up to, and we all of us fail of perfection, we want our children inculcated with these same principles. Yet when the children are taken off, in their separate bus loads, always to a place quite separate from the school, lest the Zorach decision be violated, what clearer way could there be of saying to them that religion is in one pocket and the everyday affairs of the world in another, and much larger, pocket?

Further, released time makes religion a "subject" like any other subject, which it is not. It is true that instruction is necessary. Protestants should know the Bible, or at least something of what is in it. Catholics are taught Christian doctrine without Bible reading (and they have a lot to learn since their religion is more complex than that of Protestants). Jews have to be taught the history and the meaning of their tradition. But all this, though it demands definite hours of instruction, just as do reading, writing and arithmetic, and history and science, is completely different from these studies in that it runs right through everything. We do not wish our children *merely* to know that there are four Gospels, Mat-

thew, Mark, Luke and John, or that Seder commemorates the
delivery of their ancestors from bondage in Egypt; we want
this information to be part of an attitude to life, of a tradition, that is understood and maintained as an ideal by everybody, by their parents and also by the arithmetic teacher and
the science teacher. A secular school can provide religious
instruction, but only in an atomized way. It can never provide a faith, a something to live by, a faith that is, if not
practiced to perfection by everyone, at least taken for
granted like the air one breathes.

Many years ago Americans were brought up on the Mc-
Guffey readers. This famous series of textbooks was started
in 1836. Generations of Americans were taught from them,
and they continued in use until well into this century, until
the days when John Dewey's ideas began to take hold. The
McGuffey readers leaned heavily on morals. The first reader
had "Ma-ry had a lit-tle lamb" and "Twin-kle, twin-kle little star." All the grades had instructive little stories that
ended with passages such as "Is not Frisk a fine, grateful
fellow? And does he not deserve a share of Harry's breakfast, whether he begs for it or not? And little Harry will
remember from the events of this day that kindness, even
though shown to a dog, will always be rewarded; and that
ill-nature and bad-temper are connected with nothing but
pain and disgrace." Or: "When the boys perceived how
rude and unkind their conduct appeared from another point
of view, they were very much ashamed of their thoughtless-
ness, and most of them had the manliness to apologize to
their teacher for what they had done."

This was the kind of thing that turned out in the nineteenth century those "inner directed" characters who seemed

to have a built-in gyroscope, for they had a terribly strong feeling, deep inside them, of what was *right*.

Our modern kids have to be "adjusted." The ill-adjusted child is unhappy, certainly, so let us make all the kids adjusted to their environment. Let us not insist too strongly on "right" and "wrong," for these are Absolutes, of the Old-Fashioned Kind. And besides, people who have such ideas built into them are apt to develop Guilt Feelings, and we all know how uncomfortable these are. Especially let us avoid giving a child any idea that things can be right, or wrong, irrespective of the environment, so that if the environment isn't right, he can go ahead and change it. Whatever the environment is, the kids must adjust to it. So they become "outer directed," following other people all the time. That is, they become sheep.

They also, in some cases, become beatniks. And many, many more, who do not actually grow the beard, have the same haunting feeling that they cannot find a Meaning in Life. Many, many adults feel unsatisfied, and realize that there is a deep lack of something important in their lives, something that our modern education, with its utter relativity of morals, cannot possibly provide.

The nineteenth century, for all its firm moral tone, was also characterized by hypocrisy. The school children must have poked fun constantly at the smugness of little Johnny in the third-grade reader, and the self-righteousness of the noble sentiments in the eighth. There is less hypocrisy now. But only because there is less understanding of what the ultimate standards of virtue actually are. Hypocrisy has been described as "the homage that vice pays to virtue." Nobody wants hypocrisy for its own sake, but the method we have taken to get rid of it (or rather to reduce it, for we still have hypocrisy of our own kind) has been like throwing away the baby with the bath.

How many students cheat in school or in college? What do the honest ones think when they read in the newspapers that their elders have been encouraged to cheat on television programs? How many girls get pregnant in high school? I am not one for statistics, and I have not bothered to find the answer to this, since in any case no one can know the much larger number of boys and girls who, while avoiding unwanted consequences, have had full sexual experience, many times, in the lower grades of high school. Many parents are perturbed by this, and they ought logically to welcome a kind of school that aims to inculcate strong moral standards, and they should realize that this is the reason for a certain prudish quality in the majority of church schools, a quality that is often regarded as worthy only of Mrs. Grundy. And the Catholic high schools usually are not co-educational. Is there any law that boys and girls, at the age of puberty, have to be educated together?

If there is something to be said, in general, for a certain amount of religion in education—and *in* education, permeating right through it, and not applied on the top as a separate "subject"—there is a special reason in this country why Catholics need religious schools more than Protestants do. This is because it is a Protestant country, and Protestant habits of mind are about us all the time—they form a constant atmosphere. We are, of course, a deeply Christian country. It is true we have a Jewish minority, but its culture does not make the climate of opinion. Our offices, most of our stores, and many other facilities are closed legally on Sundays, not, as in Israel, on Saturdays. No other religion has any influence to speak of on our ways of living. We do not practice, nor even countenance, polygamy. We do not have the streak of fatalism that often arises, as a by-product of the prevailing religion, in the East. No sacred cows roam our streets. Fakirs are extremely rare in our country, and they do not exhibit their mortifications in public. There are exceedingly few mosques, and from them the voice of the muezzin does not call publicly to the faithful at nightfall. No stigma attaches to eating and drinking in the daytime during Ramadan. The shops do not sell prayer wheels except as curiosities. The totem poles are in museums (or open-air museums). Our public buildings and our public meetings do not have huge pictures of Marx, Lenin and the present-day leaders of the "peace loving" nations. But Christmas is a legal holiday for all. The department stores and the liquor stores and the manufacturers of greeting cards do a huge business, but anyone who thinks that, for this reason, Christmas is purely "commercialized" and is not a religious festival, misses the point. For if there were (or if there is) any genuine, popular religious festival, our Christmas, commercial as it is, is exactly what it would be like.

Profoundly Christian this country certainly is, but no one could possibly say that its fundamental institutions and habits of mind are Catholic Christian. Corpus Christi is a day like any other day, and there are no public religious processions. Saints' days are not observed, except St. Patrick's, and that has become a national rather than a religious feast. Roadside shrines are few. But in many states the liquor laws are highly restrictive, and so are the *mores*. Posters carrying Bible quotations can be seen on our roadsides and in the subway in New York (but in Boston, the Hail Mary). In this Protestant atmosphere the Protestant Christian finds things easier than any other religious group. For him, released time may not be too unacceptable. His children will receive the necessary instruction, in suitable premises, and as for that general acceptance of Protestant Christian ideas, which is also necessary to supplement the religious instruction, that is in any case provided by the prevailing climate of opinion.

But the Catholic has the problem of providing a Catholic Christian atmosphere for his children in a Protestant Christian country. No Protestant has any conception of this problem. For a Protestant atmosphere is essentially, inherently, anti-Catholic (and *vice versa*). Protestants are usually completely and sublimely unaware of attitudes that, to them, seem as natural as water to drink, but are felt by Catholics as a constant irritation. To give only one example: a certain very important historical movement, dating from the sixteenth century, is regularly referred to as the "Reformation." The very name used for this—and it is used casually, as if taking it for granted—makes an implication which, in the Catholic view, is untrue. You do not "reform" anything by smashing it to pieces!

In this atmosphere, Catholics have set up their own system of schools, 9,400 elementary schools and 2,310 secondary schools. And since they establish and run these schools entirely out of their own money, except for trifling fringe benefits in some states only, this amounts to a saving to the American taxpayer of what it would cost to educate some four million pupils, which might be put at 3 billion dollars, every year.

And yet parochial schools are sometimes referred to as a "threat" to the public schools! An example, from a Columbia Teachers' College Conference on Rural Education: "From an educational, democratic and financial viewpoint, duplicate education systems are wasteful and inherently undemocratic. The expansion of duplicate school systems on a sectional and nation-wide scale constitutes a very grave threat to the continuing progress and improvement of the democratic school system." All right! So there is a certain inefficiency in building, say, a high school for four thousand pupils and a separate one for one thousand pupils, instead of having one building large enough for five thousand pupils, but is that *really* the important point? And as for a "threat" that turns out to be a three billion dollar saving, it is difficult to understand the "logic" on which such a remark can be based! Making an attempt to penetrate to the thought behind it, perhaps it could be expressed like this: "Public schools, providing free education available to everyone, are a great expression of our democracy. But democracy in education demands that it be *the same for everyone.* Therefore parochial schools, providing a different kind of education, are a threat to the public schools." But if anyone thinks that education, in order to be democratic, must be the same for everyone, then it would be more logical to forbid any other kind of school altogether. This would be harsh, but it would avoid a certain suspicion of hypocrisy in an attitude which amounts to saying, "We do not like your schools, and think them a 'threat' to our schools, but you may have them provided you pay for them yourselves, and continue to be taxed for our schools."

In some places in the United States—Watertown, Ohio,

and Jasper, Indiana, are two examples—there are schools which are referred to by P.O.A.U. as "captive schools." In these places, the great majority of the population is Catholic. The inequity of taxing the Catholics to provide only schools that they thoroughly dislike becomes too glaring, and a more reasonable solution is arrived at in practice: the public school becomes a Catholic school, with nuns as the teachers, a crucifix in every classroom, Hail Mary before every lesson, and Mass on holy days of obligation. This is contrary to the Constitution, as at present interpreted, and points up extremely clearly the necessity of finding some way in which public education can more closely reflect the wishes of the public.

What should be done, of course, is to allocate funds for education in proportion to the demand for different kinds of education—or at least roughly in this proportion—or at the very least to make some attempt to provide, with public funds, education which is not all at one extreme of the range of public requirement. But once again, before considering the feasibility of this (though it undoubtedly would be feasible, if we *really* wanted to do any such thing), there are still a few more important questions of principle to be examined.

"Congress shall make no law respecting an establishment of religion." This principle can be made to lead to the present state of affairs by making special interpretations of it on two points: (1) that, although the Bill of Rights only speaks of establishing "religion," it can be deemed that a church-related school is sufficiently close to a church so that the prohibition applies; and (2) that the prohibition not only covers setting up an established religion, as in England, but also forbids the State from aiding all religions on a proportionate basis. With regard to the first point, strict logic might say that a school is not a church; a priest if he were also a teacher would be on the public payroll, but would be taken off the moment he ceased teaching (a secular subject) and went back to being only a priest. But strict logic is not the only consideration, in a democracy, which takes account of people's feelings, and in this matter extremely strong feelings are involved. But if we accept (1) and relax (2), then the State can support church schools provided there is more than one type of church school to be supported. But if there were *only one* religious group that was not entirely satisfied with the kind of education customarily provided at public expense, this group would not be able to obtain any public money for its schools. And the same result would follow if the church schools were quite predominantly, say 99 per cent, of one denomination, with entirely insignificant numbers of any other.

On the other hand, suppose there were several large groups of denominational schools, not all of the same size, but with some two or three major groups not too unequal. One might imagine 50 per cent of the population content with the kind of education provided by "public" schools, and three largish denominations representing 20 per cent, 15 per cent and 10 per cent of the population, with 5 per cent "other." We are supposing that the Constitution is interpreted to mean that the State can certainly support church schools, provided it does so without any favoritism, just as is done with chaplains in the armed forces. No one could demand that State support be withdrawn from all church schools simply because the two largest denominations were not precisely equal. (Even if they were precisely equal at one time, they might not stay that way.) A liberal interpretation of the Constitution would not be violated on account of the fact that the largest of the church groups would obtain more State money than the next largest, proportionately to its size.

But as if there were not already enough difficulties in this troublesome matter, the actual state of affairs is intermediate between these two cases. Of a total of forty-two million children in elementary and high schools throughout the country (1958), nearly 4.5 million, or 10.6 per cent, are in church schools. Of these, as we have noted, a little over four million are in the Catholic parochial schools, while Jewish schools and those of a considerable number of Protestant sects amount to 366,000. The largest non-Catholic church school system is that of the Missouri Lutheran Synod, with 130,000 pupils in about one thousand elementary schools and 7,000 in thirteen high schools; the next largest is the Seventh Day Adventists, with 55,000 pupils in about eleven hundred schools. Of the total pupils in elementary and secondary church schools, the percentage in Catholic parochial schools is 91.8 per cent, with 8.2 per cent in non-Catholic religious schools. Which principle applies?

It is very easy for anyone who has an intense desire to prevent the Catholic schools from getting any State support to conclude from these figures that the first principle applies, that the percentage of Roman Catholic pupils is so overwhelming that all the others, from the Missouri Lutheran Synod down, are "entirely insignificant." But . . . there are some "buts." In the first place, such a decision would penalize Catholics for the very energy and self-sacrifice with which they have built up and supported their most extensive school system. If they had been far less energetic about this, they would be in a *better* position to ask for help in what they are doing! But, to repeat, Catholics need church schools more than Protestants do, for they have the problem, incomprehensible to American Protestants, of bringing up their children in one faith in a culture which is saturated with a somewhat different faith.

Again, the figures 91.8 per cent and 8.2 per cent represent pupils in actual church schools. They do not in the least reflect the proportions of the various religions in the adult population. These proportions are hard to measure accurately, but they may be roughly estimated as something like 66 per cent Protestant, 26 per cent Catholic, 3.2 per cent Jewish, and the remaining 4.8 per cent "other" or noncommittal. (These figures are presented without splitting certain hairs that could be split, as to whether Eastern Orthodox counts as "Protestant" or Episcopalianism as "Catholic.") Protestants have been much less energetic than Catholics in setting up church schools because, in a Protestant climate of opinion, they need them less. This does not mean that they actually *like* the public schools, but only that they object to them less than the Catholics do. And since, in this culture, an entirely secular education, with released time, is only moderately repugnant to Protestants, the great majority have accepted it rather than go to the great expense of organizing special schools in addition to those paid for out of their taxes. At the same time the great majority of them have loudly proclaimed their enthusiasm for the extreme interpretation of separation of Church and State, according to which *no* church group receives any aid for its schools. But suppose—for we are still talking "supposes" in order to arrive at principles—we were to have the *proportional system* (let us call it that for a convenient handle). The number of Protestant church schools would then take a very sharp rise. All manner of Bible-type schools would arise all over the Bible belt, and secular education would be maintained for the secular few. Many people would not regard this prospect with enthusiasm. But it would be democratic in a very practical way. It would be making at least some attempt to provide people with education of the kind that they actually want for their children.

Then there is the question of feasibility—could all this be done? This question has two parts, fiscal and organizational. Both of them are extremely thorny.

Just *how* is the money to be divided? So far, we have been speaking as if allocating education funds under the proportional system were an easy matter, but it is not. Here are suggested four possible ways of doing it:

1. Every time a national census is taken (every ten years) let one of the questions asked of everyone over twenty-one be: "Which type of school would you prefer to be supported by your tax money?"

This would get into federal-state trouble. For the census is conducted by the Federal Bureau of the Census, which would then have to inform the states of the way the voting went among their residents. The states would probably adopt a huffy, offended attitude, at being "told what to do with their money by the Federal Government."

2. Every time there is an election, let the same question be asked of every voter. For the states have no trouble in

placing both federal and state voting matters on the same voting machine.

3. Let the same question be asked of every taxpayer. This could be done in several ways, according to the kind of taxes involved. It would be possible to slip in this question on everyone's income-tax form—but this would involve federal-state trouble again. State income tax would not do, because it usually only begins at a much higher income level, and in any case some states do not at present have any income tax. It could be done in connection with property taxes; every such taxpayer would be invited to express his preference with regard to the allocation of school funds. This would appeal to those literal-minded persons who would reason as follows: "The public schools are usually supported mainly out of funds derived from taxes on property; it is therefore the direct payers of these taxes who should have the say on how the funds are to be spent." Against this it may be objected that even those who own no "property" contribute to the taxes indirectly, for they all pay rent, and if the taxes are higher, so are rents. And in any case, a decision such as this should be made on a basis of true democracy, not money-democracy with a property qualification for voting. But if there were any likelihood of alternative (3) being adopted, then all those in favor of the general objective to be achieved would be wise to drop this objection, for it is always difficult to convince the literal-minded.

Of the three possibilities discussed so far the following is to be noted, that the "universe" (to use the mathematician's term) within which the decision is to be made is different. In (3) it is "taxpayers" of one kind or another, in (2) it is "voters," in (1) it is "everyone over twenty-one" even if they pay no taxes other than sales tax and various indirect taxes. If it is democratic that "he who pays the piper calls the tune" then alternative (3) should be adopted. On the other hand, education is for everyone's children, and even those who have no children are concerned with the education of tomorrow's citizens and are taxed for education. There is therefore something to be said for every one of these three methods, and we could adopt any one of them according to convenience, or if any one were preferred (or the other two objected to) by any group having strong feelings on the subject.

(4) By far the simplest way of settling this matter would be on the basis of the number of pupils in the schools. If a community had five thousand pupils in secular schools, one thousand in Catholic parochial schools, and two hundred in one or more Protestant or Jewish schools, then the public funds would be allocated in exactly that proportion. This could be handled in a number of different ways as regards the details, and with good will it would soon be possible to find the most expeditious way.

But there is a strange and formidable objection to solution (4). It is this: since Catholics generally have larger families than non-Catholics, the share of the public funds which their schools would receive would be greater under (4) than under (1), (2) or (3). Plan (4) would therefore be certain to encounter strenuous opposition, which would be put forward under some specious, legalistic reasoning. Probably plan (3) is the one which would give the Catholics least, and would therefore attract most support.

Concerning any or all of these plans, or any others that might be put forward, it is extremely easy for anyone to say

"It won't work" just because it is somewhat more complicated than our present oversimplified system. When a man says "It can't be done" there are two possibilities (or rather two extremes with intergrades). One man may have tried and tried and tried and finally come sadly to the conclusion "It can't be done." Another man may say offhand, "It can't be done" or "It won't work" at the very first suggestion of any proposal, before he has taken any time to examine its feasibility. This man is subject to the suspicion that what he really thinks is "I don't want it to be done."

The proposal suggested here is by no means of excessive complexity. It involves somewhat more trouble than our present way of doing things; somewhat more bureaucratic work, somewhat more red tape. Red tape is not desirable for its own sake, but a little extra organization and accountkeeping may be necessary to achieve something that is desired. But it must be desired. At present there is certainly no overwhelming public desire to achieve the proportional system (understatement of the year). That is why it is very easy to say "It won't work." It certainly wouldn't work, if there were a large number of people passionately opposed to it. But if there were a majority of people wishing to achieve it, with a minority at least willing to go along, it is clearly not beyond the wit of man to find some entirely workable solution.

The proposal is extremely elastic, and it might be accepted not as sketched above, but with modifications. (1) It might be ordained that the church schools should receive one-half (or some other fraction) of their total expenses from the State. This would discourage fly-by-night organizations from optimistically starting a school, and then finding themselves unable to keep it up. (2) The rule might be that existing schools should receive their full quota, prorated according to the number of pupils, but that the erection of a new school building should be done with public funds only for a secular school. Adherents of any sect wishing a school would have to provide the building from voluntary contributions, although thereafter, for running expenses, they would receive their proportionate share of public funds (to which they might add voluntarily if they wished). Many other modifications might be suggested, catering to every desire and whim.

How would school districts be organized? Here is another opportunity for anyone who dislikes the proportional system to say, "It wouldn't work. It is too complicated."

It would certainly make things more complicated than they are now. And in considering the matter, it is to be remarked that it would never be possible to work things out with exact mathematical precision over the whole of the country. Things do not work out with mathematical precision right now. In sparsely settled regions it is most difficult to establish school districts that do not involve excessive amounts of traveling for some of the children. Shall a one-room, one-teacher school be provided reasonably close, or a bigger, better equipped institution at a considerable distance? The proportional system divides the pupils of the country into several populations, each extending over the whole country, but differently distributed, so that one may be sparse in a region where another is dense. Difficult cases owing to fewness of pupils may occur anywhere, any way round. There would be cases where a few intensely secular parents would find it hard to organize a corresponding school, but under the proportional system they would not have any greater rights than any other groups of parents who might find themselves in the same fix. In districts where Catholics are sparse it would be hard to establish a parochial school, but this kind of hardship would present nothing new, for the situation is very familiar to Catholics as it is. Jews would have the same difficulty, as indeed they do now, in those many parts of the country where they are few. It is in any case most difficult for them to perpetuate their special culture, but at any rate in those parts of the country where there is a considerable Jewish population they would have no difficulty in founding and maintaining special Jewish schools if they wanted to—schools where they could celebrate Hanukkah without having to pretend that it is the same as Christmas. Mathematical precision would *never* be obtained. But that is no reason for not trying to come nearer to perfection, rather than further from it; for not trying to do *something* rather than nothing, for not at least trying to move away from the present "compromise" which is not a compromise at all, for it supports only one extreme at the expense not only of the other extreme but also of the middle. And as for anyone who should continue to say, "It can't be done," he should consider that there are various countries where it actually *is* done in one way or another, countries where church schools of more than one religious persuasion receive public support. Examples: Holland, England, the Irish Republic, and several provinces of Canada, notably Quebec, where it has long been the understood thing that both Catholic and Protestant schools are supported by public funds.

If we could have the proportional system in the United

States, some changes would probably be noted in the pattern
of our Protestant schools. There are at present more than
three thousand such schools, supported by no less than
twenty-eight denominations. Under the proportional system
such schools would undoubtedly increase in number. But
there would also be a need for schools of a less sectarian
character. Not everyone who is a Protestant is closely identified with any one sect. Many communities have a non-de-
nominational community church. There would also arise a
demand for a corresponding community-church school. Not
every Protestant parent wants a school which is dripping
with sectarian piety. There would be a great demand for
schools in which a little Bible-reading on the premises, perhaps even some mild hymn-singing, would actually be permitted. And if some groups required special instruction on
released time—would it be too much to ask that it be permitted on the same premises? What principle would be violated?

What principle, indeed, governs this matter? What principle is being invoked in insisting upon such an extreme
interpretation of separation of Church and State? The question is a heated one; it always generates heat in any discussion. Perhaps this is because the alleged principle isn't the
genuinely felt one. It may be that the following little anec-
dote from the history of Church-State relations in this country, unimportant though it is in itself, may help to illustrate
the matter:

In the city of New Orleans, at the junction of Harrison
Avenue and Canal Street, there is a statue of Frances Xavier
Cabrini, a benefactress of the city, who had founded an or-
phanage. The inscription on the statue says that it is "in

honor and recognition of the outstanding services rendered to the community in the field of child care and for her effort and sacrifices during the Yellow Fever epidemics of 1897 and 1905." So far so good, but it happens that Mother Cabrini (a) was a nun and (b) has been canonized by the Roman Catholic Church—she is a Saint! And so, sure enough, a small group of citizens were so infuriated by this that they determined to have the statue removed. They started a legal action declaring that to place a statue of such a person on city property was a violation of the First Amendment, the separation of Church and State! The court rejected their suit, holding that the statue was not erected because of its religious nature, but simply on account of that orphanage, which still flourishes, and the good work in the yellow fever epidemics. And so the statue is still there.

I have never heard that there has been any objection to the statue, outside Borough Hall in Brooklyn, of Henry Ward Beecher because he was a Protestant minister, nor have I bothered to find out how many other statues, on municipal or even state property, commemorate ministers, rabbis or elders of the Mormon Church. It was not proposed, in New Orleans, to desecrate (perhaps "desecularize" is the word) the city property by the public exhibit of a cross (much less a crucifix) or a Star of David. These are exclusive symbols of religious groups, and should not be treated in such a manner. The proposal simply concerned a statue of a person who had done the sort of thing for the city that qualifies for a statue, anywhere in the world, and to object to it on the alleged ground of separation of Church and State is nothing short of ridiculous.

It would seem clear that the principle violated is a rather

simple one—*never let the Catholics get anything*. For such is the dislike and fear that the Catholic Church arouses that this principle is widely accepted. Widely accepted, but not so widely acknowledged. We have the spectacle of more than two dozen Protestant denominations running schools; some few of them accept bus rides, possibly lunches, such fringe benefits as the Catholic school sometimes get, but the great majority of them (some Episcopalians and some Jewish groups are exceptions) never demand or expect state aid on a proportional basis, indeed regard it as utterly heinous to do so. Is it being too darkly suspicious to suggest that the real reason is that if they got it, the Catholics would get it too? For if this is not the reason, then the fact that all these denominations interpret Church-State separation in such an extreme manner, so contrary to their own interests, is quite without explanation.

The situation is distressing, and has distressing by-products. It makes Catholics shy away from the "liberal" organizations such as the American Civil Liberties Union, for "liberal" is construed to mean "extreme interpretation of separation of Church and State" and Catholics cannot go along with that. And it drives Catholic parishes to frantic raffles and bingo games, practically making a gambling den out of the parish house, in the desperate struggle to raise money to keep the schools going.

And so what can be done about it? Even those who are in favor of a more liberal interpretation of Church-State separation must realize that change can come only very slowly. To change a Supreme Court interpretation takes many years of very gradual change in public opinion. It was done that way for the old "separate but equal" interpretation in the matter of race relations. Those who are contented with the present state of affairs can have confidence, for a change would seem to be highly unlikely in the present climate of opinion.

Perhaps we can arrive at a clearer realization of what our problems really are. We are committed to a pluralist society, one that provides freedom and equal treatment for all religions. But it is most difficult to realize that different religions actually are different, and that one of the ways in which these differences express themselves is in requiring different schools—not different in instruction, but different in atmosphere, in background. Separate sectarian schools are often denounced as being a "divisive influence." Certainly they are a divisive influence! The fundamental principle of a pluralist society is that it *permits* such divisive things as differences in religion. Some even go so far as to say that these divisive sectarian schools are "un-American." Is uniformity a fundamental principle of "Americanism?" There may be some who suppose that it is. These people, if there are such, have turned their back on a pluralist society.

We manage our pluralist society with only a moderate amount of friction, but then our problems are so much easier than those of some other countries. A classic example of a country with far more difficult problems is the large area formerly known as India, now divided along religious lines into India and Pakistan. But we have no clash anywhere near as severe as that between Hindus and Moslems. All we have, except for extremely small minorities, is Catholics, Christians of other denominations, and Jews. This is not exactly three religions, but two, for Catholics and Protestants are all Christians. And if ever there were two religions which *ought* to be able to get along together, they are Christianity and Judaism. In practice there is often friction, or worse, but it is invariably the fault of the Christians.

If we are to get down to true principles, that is, truly felt principles, whether they are warranted or not, then perhaps a person who has fear of the Catholic Church as one of his principles ought to say so. When he denies that a Catholic has the right to obtain, for his tax money, a school that is acceptable to him, perhaps he should do this openly for fear of the Catholics, rather than speciously in the name of "civil liberties." For anti-Catholicism is entirely different from anti-Semitism. If a person is anti-Semitic, and you ask him his reasons, he can give none that are not utter rubbish. But if a person is anti-Catholic he *can* give his reasons. And as long as a person is giving reasons, reasonable discussion is still possible.

Possible—but extremely difficult. For any discussion encounters misunderstanding and suspicion on many levels. "Public aid to parochial schools! Then you don't believe in separation of Church and State!"—and it is necessary to explain that the proposal is for public aid to *all* church schools, and that the discussion does not concern separation of Church and State, but the interpretation of this principle, whether we should adopt the *extreme interpretation,* as at present, or the *liberal interpretation,* which is much more permissive; that the proposal is not to break down the Wall of Separation, nor to make a single chip in its excellent masonry, but simply suggests that it has been built in the wrong place. The Wall would be far more easily defended if it immured less territory.

On a deeper level the discussion touches the whole question of what *is* democracy, and how we shall achieve democracy in education. The concept of "democracy" is complex, and of its various components some pull one way, some the other, in regard to education. An important component of our idea of democracy is the equality of everyone. We do not have a built-in aristocracy, and no one is treated any differently because he is a duke or any kind of lord. We have moneyed people, and working people, but money comes and money goes, and our aristocracy of money is flexible, its membership changes. It is democratic, according to this part of our concept of democracy, for children of all classes to rub shoulders together. It is in this sense, and this sense only, that private church schools are undemocratic. It is felt very strongly by some that these schools encourage separateness instead of togetherness. But nothing encourages separateness as much as the *pay* private schools, those that are set up not primarily in order to have a religious atmosphere in education but for a better *quality* in education, by paying the teachers more and having smaller classes (some of these schools, but by no means all, combine both objectives). These are as undemocratic as can be.

The other understanding of democracy in education considers the feelings of the parents. For parents have strong feelings about the education of their children, and it is the feelings of the parents that count. Parents (and also non-parents) pay taxes for schools, and it is not democratic that *all* the education tax money should be applied to only *one* kind of school.

But then our present way of doing things does not achieve democracy in the "togetherness" sense either. If democracy in education demands that all our children should rub shoulders together, then we should not be permissive towards any separate, church-related schools that certain groups of people are willing to pay for, but should prohibit them. And certainly there would be something to be said for forbidding the fancy Ivy-League "prep" schools in which the rich are allowed to buy out of democracy. The money that the parents of prep-school children pay should be taxed away from them and applied to the improvement of the public schools.

Other disagreements lie deeper still. Often they are deeply felt rather than brought up clearly to the conscious level. To mention only one, many Protestants have a feeling, which is not often clearly articulated, but which might be expressed as follows: "Catholics never really understand the true meaning of democracy; consequently their schools fail to indoctrinate the children properly." To which a Catholic might reply that in this country the idea of democracy often takes on an aura of irrational mystique, and sometimes even assumes some of the characteristics of a religion. A Catholic does not mistake *vox populi* for *vox Dei.*

Both sides are to blame. Protestants and secularists are to be blamed for the complacency with which they accept, for *their* schools, the tax money of Catholics (and some few Protestants and Jews) to whom the godless public schools are totally unacceptable; and for the smugness with which they say in effect, "The public schools are open to all. You don't *have* to build and run your own schools. And there are other fields in which people get taxed, occasionally, for facilities they don't themselves use—so why should you worry!" Catholics are to be blamed for the way in which they put their case. They are apt to gripe exclusively about the injustice done to *them.* Their case would be far more sympathetically listened to if they had some thought for other religious groups who run church schools. They should always make it clear that they seek the application of public funds to *all* church schools. They should emphasize that they never expect for their schools any more money than corresponds, proportionately, to the amount of money they themselves have paid in taxes, so that nobody will be taxed in any amount "for opinions which he disbelieves" as Thomas Jefferson feared. As it is, the Catholic pronouncements, from the bishops down to the laity, sound like "gimme, gimme, gimme." They behave like a pressure group, and it is natural that they are feared like one.

And so it goes. It shows every prospect of going on for some considerable time. The dialogue should continue, slow and difficult though it may be. Meanwhile the present state of affairs, which is not too intolerable, will continue. There is room for plenty of improvement, but this requires discussion and, if possible, understanding. Throughout there is needed one special ingredient, one that Protestants, Catholics and Jews can all supply; one mystery ingredient—Charity.

6 : *This Cold Religious War*

CULTURAL ANTHROPOLOGISTS have done a most creditable job of propagating the idea that other cultures than our own are not crazy, but deserve a sympathetic understanding.

Cultural anthropologists travel all over the world, and study any culture that is in existence now (even though it may be rapidly disappearing). They do not travel in time. Historians do all the time traveling that is possible. But historians have been much less successful, if indeed they have tried at all, in convincing people that cultures that existed *in the past* are deserving of any sympathetic understanding. This is because of the idea of Progress, which asserts that, as time flows steadily along, human affairs become better and better. A conclusion from this is that going further and further into the past things become worse and worse. This may be true in some respects, but it is not true in all.

We learn in history that there was a time—long since gone —when people were so crude and lacking in understanding as to engage in religious wars.

We are engaged right now in a war. A "cold" war, it is true, but with the hideous possibility of its becoming hot

144

at any moment. Our *mores* utterly forbid a religious war, and therefore this has to be described as a political war. For it is deemed that we have made far too much "progress," we are much too civilized, to be engaged in a religious war at any temperature, hot or cold.

If we move backwards along the path by which our culture came into being, we will find ourselves in Europe, and in that very large and little understood period of time that is known as "medieval." And it may not be too much of an exaggeration to say that, in that very ill defined period, a war *had* to be a religious war. Even if its objects were purely political, it was necessary to find some formula by which it could be palmed off as a religious war, or at least a war for some moral principle, such as putting the "rightful" king on the throne. For, hundreds of years ago, if a man thought that things were being done very badly and should be done better, he would write a book about theology. In the nineteenth and twentieth centuries, if a man had this splendid, nay divine, discontent, he would write a book about politics or economics.

If a country deliberates whether to go to war or not (by whatever means the deliberation is done, according to its political constitution) there is only *one* question to be asked, and that is: Is this war just? A just war is justified. An unjust war is not. The *question* at least is simple. The answer will in all cases involve appalling complications, with usually a considerable measure both of justice and of injustice on each side, but the resolution of the complications has to be made in terms of one measure only, justice.

Our *mores* recognize this, in a limited way. We seek to find the aggressor. We vow that our country will never become an aggressor. If all countries adopted this attitude, there could never be any war, for a war must be started by someone, and the country that starts the war is the aggressor. It is not necessarily an inherent objection to this doctrine that it is exceedingly difficult to find out who did start any given war, for *any* principle on this subject is bound to be exceedingly difficult of application to practical cases, and yet, in spite of this, we must have principles. Nor is it a fatal objection to this principle that it can be applied speciously; almost any principle can be misapplied and perverted. Under the "no-aggression" principle, when two rapacious countries get into a cold-war situation, a premium is granted to that rapacious country which more skillfully jockeys or needles the other into committing an act which can be construed as "war."

If ever a war was justified, in recent times, it was the Second World War. It was for the purpose of destroying Hitler and the Nazis before they conquered the whole world. It succeeded so brilliantly that it is now becoming somewhat difficult to realize how intense was the emergency, how imminent the danger. Once we were embarked upon this war, all the resources of propaganda, required for working up the necessary enthusiasm in a democratic population, were engaged in telling the truth about the Nazis, their ruthlessness, their anti-Semitism, their paganism, their cruelty, and, above all, their plans for world domination and the likelihood of their achieving this. But before the war began, its outbreak had to be justified in the more limited sense required by our customs, that of "aggression," of "being the first to break the peace." England and France, after seeing one country after another swallowed by the Nazis, had to take a strong stand at some point, upon a good pretext or a bad one. After many missed opportunities it was necessary for Chamberlain to "guarantee" the next country on the list, which happened to be Poland, even though the "guarantee" could mean no more than that, long after Poland had been overrun, it might eventually be liberated for the benefit of such Poles as survived. In this country, where isolationism was extremely strong, Roosevelt had the luck to see his policy of needling Japan become brilliantly successful when the Japanese were so utterly foolish as to attack not only the British possessions in the Far East but also Pearl Harbor. Germany declared war on us the next day. "Ratso, Fatso and Japso"—this was one slogan in the propaganda that then sprang up overnight. For the people had to be convinced, not only of the real reasons why we were fighting Hitler, Mussolini and the Japanese, but also that our enemies, powerful as they might be, could in a way be looked upon as slightly contemptible, slightly ridiculous.

We fought World War II for reasons that were as genuine as could possibly be, to rid the world of a monstrous and threatening evil. We understood these reasons, as is our habit, in political terms. They can also be understood in other ways.

By a great effort of imagination let us try to suppose that World War II had been fought in the medieval period. What would we read, in the archaic accounts, of that personage, that ruler in the Germanies, called Adolphus Hitlerus? We would find him described as an heretic, most vile and abominable in the sight of the Lord, who stinketh in the nostrils of all true believers. His misdeeds would be described entirely in theological terms. Prize exhibits of infamy would

be all his speeches in which he said anything about God—
and there are quite a few such, for Hitler, for all his enormity,
was apparently not an atheist. God was not only, as with
Frederick the Great, on the side of the big battalions; he
was invariably with the Germans. God would support a suitable order in this world, that is to say with the master race
firmly in the saddle and the various *Untermenschen,* down
to the Jews, in their respective lower stations. One feels that
God was blond and blue-eyed. To make an appalling pun,
Hitlerism would be described as the "Aryan heresy."

There was something about the Nazis that resembled a
religion—perverted, horrible, though not quite entirely atheist. Their youth dedication rites, their worship of health and
bodily strength (for Aryans) were often described as pagan.
Their fanaticism, their sense of mission can easily find parallels in many religions. So, too, can their intense determination
to impose an *order* on this world. It is the greatest mistake
to suppose that theirs was a cult of nihilism, that their aim
was destruction. Few countries (with the exception of course
of Communist countries) have ever been so intensely constructive. Their plan was laid down for all to read in *Mein
Kampf.* They were to *build* not only Germany but the whole
world. And they were to build it on a wrong principle—that
"Aryans" should be masters, and all others slaves.

A doctrine entirely different from this, that "all men are
created equal," is the basis of political theory in this country
and in very many others. Such a doctrine is, of course, entirely incompatible with the doctrine of Aryan supremacy.
If the Nazi doctrine had been "In Europe, Aryans are to
be supreme," the two systems could have existed simultane-
ously in different regions. They would have generated a

constant, but not necessarily explosive, mutual friction. But the ideas of the Nazis were to be of universal application. They were to prevail over the whole world. Therefore as soon as the Nazis showed a likelihood of succeeding, war was inevitable. And it had to be regarded as a political war. The equality of man is deeply built into all our political institutions. It is expressed in noble terms in our fundamental political document, the Declaration of Independence. Thus we had no difficulty in describing this war, to ourselves, as a political war.

There is no doubt about the origin of the doctrine of the equality of man. It has no conceivable origin except Christianity. The Christian tradition speaks of the "brotherhood of man." And this means not just an extended relationship, in a physiological or genealogical sense, as one might speak of the "brotherhood of dogs" or the "sisterhood of cats." This is taking the phrase as a loose way of speaking in which "brother" is used to mean "extremely distant cousin." The expression is true because presumably we are all descendants of the original mutation (or perhaps two mutations, one male and one female) by which a recognizable man evolved from an apelike ancestor. Thus we know that all human beings are connected by a remote consanguinity. This does not in the least lead to any kind of equality of man, for there may have been further mutations along the line, as a result of which some races of men became "better" than others. It is compatible with such a doctrine as the Greek idea of "natural slaves." The Christian idea goes much further than this, and speaks of men as "children of God," thereby implying not only equality (in the sense intended by the Founding Fathers of this country), but also, what is far more difficult, an obligation of mutual love. But laws and political institutions cannot prescribe love, and the political basis of this country calls for no more than the equality of all men before the law. This was entirely sufficient for a political war against Hitler's Germany.

Suppose, again, that the last World War had been fought in that dim, historical period when political institutions were thought of, not as expressions of the habit of thought, the intellectual fashion, of a people—changeable (slowly, not quickly) and therefore capable of contradictory positions at different times—but as resting on fixed ideas, such as the brotherhood of man in the Christian sense. Suppose that a writer of that time, after describing Hitler the heretic, were to give an account of the position of the Western nations in this war. He would have no difficulty in contrasting the Christian idea of the Western world, for which they were fighting, with the terrible heresy raging in Germany. The entire struggle would be described in religious terms, which we would probably consider a piece of hypocrisy. Yet the description would be true.

All wars are either religious wars, or "have—have-not" wars, that is to say, wars waged by the have-not's against the have's (or else by the have's in order to have more). Most wars partake of both qualities.

World War II, against the Nazis, can fairly easily be seen to be at least partly a religious war. But to see our present war, this cold war, in this way demands quite a stretch of our mental muscles, conditioned as they are by our culture, to the point of Pavlovian automation, never to question that "Any war in which we are engaged, even coldly, cannot be a religious war." The Russian regime is known to be strongly anti-religious. How can an anti-religion be a religion?

But what is a religion? In a superficial view, and if we confine our attention to this country, the question seems easy to answer. If we extend our range of attention to other countries, including those with which we might conceivably be at war, we encounter perplexities. Religions are different—it is extremely hard to realize how *different* they are—especially since our *mores* prescribe an almost compulsive tendency to think of them as all but identical! It may be profitable, for understanding our relations with other cultures, if we make a careful, rather than superficial, examination of the innocent-sounding question: What *is* a religion?

The legal status of any religion in this country is that of a sort of club. As was noted in the previous chapter, we have three main religions, Protestant Christianity, Catholic Christianity, and Judaism (there are some others, with smaller numbers of adherents). It is characteristic of Protestant Christianity to be divided into a large number of different groups, or sects. Catholic Christianity does not have this characteristic in the least. Judaism shares it to a slight extent. Thus there are a number of these "clubs" that a person can belong to, or to none at all. The word "club" is not quite appropriate, even by analogy, because in our culture it is regarded as axiomatic that these "sects" or "clubs" are mutually exclusive. A man cannot belong to two religions at once—or so we think.

Now it may be noted right away that this axiom, which cannot be questioned in our culture, and which also holds in a good many other cultures, nevertheless does not hold universally. In Japan it is possible for a man to be both a Bud-

dhist and a Shintoist, and yet Buddhism and Shintoism are
both thought of as religions.

Christianity and Islam both claim to be universal religions.
Christians must preach the gospel to the ends of the earth,
baptizing all converts in the name of the Father, and of the
Son, and of the Holy Ghost. Islam insists that *all* men *are*
Moslems, whether they know it or not. All men must be
brought to realize this, by the sword if necessary. Moham-
med himself led an army in the field.

Buddhism, too, is a universal religion, in a somewhat different way. Karma and the Wheel of Life apply to all men,
and to animals too, indeed to all forms of life. All men must
escape eventually from the Wheel of Life by practicing re-
nunciation, by the Eightfold Path taught by the Buddha.
Buddhism does not send out either armies or intense, passionate missionaries. Even without these, it has spread, geographically, far from its place of origin in India, and it
exercises a considerable, sometimes a controlling, influence
over *mores* in various places from Ceylon to Japan.

The main religions of India, roughly grouped together and
referred to under the name of Hinduism, are different again.
Christianity, Islam, and Buddhism are alike in this, that there
is a more or less coherent, and more or less unchangeable,
body of doctrine that one can point to as what the religion
is. This is clearest, and most notably true, in Catholic Christianity and Islam; in Islam it is particularly easy to see because it is all frozen in the Book written by the Prophet, the
Koran. But Hinduism is not *one* religion in the sense in which
each of the others has a certain unity. It is a group of sub-
religions, shall we say, that hold some things in common and
are compatible with one another so that in some parts of

India Siva is chiefly worshipped, in others Krishna, and many other gods by different local or caste groups—and yet all the gods are recognized to be different expressions of one god, who is not, as in the Christian belief, the *creator* of the universe, but in a sense *is* the universe. Hinduism does not send out missionaries, and it has achieved no more than a negligible influence outside of India. And yet in spite of all this it is, in a certain way, a universal religion, but in a different way from Christianity and Islam, on the one hand, and from Buddhism on the other. It *swallows* other religions. It can always accept a new god into its pantheon. (In this respect it resembles the religion, such as it was, of the ancient Greeks and Romans.) And there are some religions that allow themselves to be assimilated without making difficulties. (The Romans, in their conquests, usually met with this, but the Druids were an exception, and also, most notably, the Jews.) There are attempts being made in India, right now, to make Jesus Christ one of the gods, that are all expressions of the one God. Even Jawaharlal Nehru has been voted a god—he declined the honor. But it may be noted that in some four hundred years of close contact, Hinduism has made not the slightest progress in assimilating Islam.

One religion, extremely important in the modern world, is not universalist—Judaism. It has this rather unusual feature, that membership in the group goes by descent. The only reason for being Jewish is that a person's parents were Jewish (or one of the parents). Now, of course it is *usually* true that the children of Christians are Christian, and the children of Moslems, Moslem. But it is not *inherently* so. The Jewish religion will sometimes take in proselytes (at some periods of history more than at others; at this period of history rather few). But the proselytes are required to *marry into the group*. This is very different from the situation in Christianity and Islam, where converts are eagerly sought, but do not have to marry into the previous group. A Christian convert should marry a Christian, but it is permissible to marry a Christian convert. In times gone by it was quite common for an entire tribe or nation to embrace Christianity. The converts could then marry one another, and there was not the slightest obligation of intermarriage with any other group of Christians. But a Jewish proselyte should marry into the main group of the descendants of Abraham, so that his descendants are descendants of Abraham. The complex set of dietary laws, the ritual purifications, the prohibition of work on the Sabbath, the whole apparatus of Orthodox Judaism, the whole Mosaic law, are *not* laws of universal validity, but are intended to be binding *only* on God's chosen people, the descendants of Abraham. There is nothing resembling this in any other of the main religions in the world today.

And so—what is a religion? Such very different kinds of belief, and behavior, are comprised under "religion" that we might find that the Russians have a religion after all—if the meaning of the word could be stretched sufficiently. And it *should* be stretched. We use words to describe reality. But the complexity of words is not equal to the complexity of reality. Words are our servants, not our masters, and we can make them do what we want. We go wrong in our thinking by misunderstanding reality according to the meager and inadequate categories of thought provided by our words. If words and the true state of affairs "out there" fail to correspond, it is not reality that must be distorted. We must make new words or change the meanings of old ones, whichever causes less confusion. We may have to find an extended meaning of the word "religion" in order to cover the complexities of our modern world.

We ordinarily think of a man's religion as the form taken by his relationship with God. For a man cannot have much relationship with his Creator entirely by himself, in a social vacuum, and without any contact with and influence from others who have gone before him and have shaped out several great traditions, within any of which a man may develop a relation with his God. These great traditions we think of as various approaches to the same end. We exaggerate the resemblances, and we disregard the differences.

This "definition" of religion, this way of thinking about what it *is* (it would be better to think about what various religions *are*) is prevalent in our culture. Since our culture has been, in recent times, astonishingly successful, and is at present "dominant," this definition has gone a long way towards being accepted over the whole world. Again, since it is a product of our culture, it is cast in the Judeo-Christian way of thinking, which has shaped our culture. It speaks of "God" and "man," with a certain antithesis between them, the Creator and the creature. It requires a slight distortion to be applicable to Hinduism, in which the relation between God and the whole universe, including man, is decidedly different. And it breaks down entirely for one important and extremely admirable religion, Buddhism, in which there is apparently no God at all, nothing but the Wheel of Life, Karma, and the ultimately attainable Nirvana.

This popular understanding of what is meant by religion is at least right in this, that it speaks of an *individual* and *personal* matter for each man. Everyone must decide, by himself and with his own thinking, what God is and what must be his relationship to Him. Each man will consider, of course, what others have thought and said on the subject before deciding on so weighty a matter, but his decision is personal and entirely his own.

It is also part of the popular understanding that each man's decision is personal also in this sense, that it is a *private* matter, of no concern to others (except perhaps close friends or relatives who may have strong feelings, one way or another), and above all of no concern to the State. The State is to be concerned with secular matters, and is to take no account of a man's decision in regard to his relation with God.

In this respect the popular understanding does not seem to reflect realities as they have been in history and as they are today.

We commonly speak of religion, not only as a characteristic of individuals—as, this man is an Episcopalian, that man was brought up as a Methodist but has gone in strongly for Yoga, or Zen Buddhism—but as a characteristic of whole countries. Spain is a Catholic country, Sweden a Protestant country, Tibet was profoundly Buddhist (perhaps of a decadent kind), Saudi Arabia is a Moslem country.

These differences between countries are not purely nominal. They do more than describe such differences as that the climate of Spain is different from that of Holland, that the Tibetans burn yak dung and put butter in their tea, and that the Swedes eat smorgasbord. They describe a certain kind of social character that each country possesses. For a religious difference between two countries may underlie important and far-reaching differences in their *mores* and habits of life, for example, the number of wives that a man may have. Other differences may be subtle, and of less vital import, as that in Israel the shops are closed on Saturday and open on Sunday, whereas the reverse is the case in Christian countries. Religion is a thing affecting a whole country, giving it a certain character.

St. Patrick converted Ireland to Christianity. That is to say, he converted the Irish. Each Irishman, apparently, made his individual choice that Christianity was better than the old paganism, and Ireland became Christian. The blessed saint did an astoundingly thorough job, for in one-and-a-half millennia since his time there has never been the faintest doubt about it—Ireland is a Christian country. St. Augustine converted England, or, rather, he converted the Saxons in the southern part of Great Britain. St. Boniface from England converted the Germans. Within a scant hundred years from the Hegira, the swords of the believers had carried Islam all over North Africa, were about to start their long ascendancy in Spain, and had also penetrated to the East to many places far distant from Arabia. Over much of this territory Islam still prevails.

Such is the language of history. It speaks of religion almost in territorial terms. "Such and such a region became Christian—this district fell to Islam—Buddhist teachings have prevailed in Ceylon." It seems to be discussing something widely different from a choice, which is made by each man individually and which is not only personal but also private, so that it is of no concern to his fellow men, either privately or publicly. Is it not possible that our view of religion as something purely personal and private covers a truth, but not the whole truth?

There is another way in which the "personal choice" theory of religion fails to reflect reality. What about the man who makes no choice at all? Those who are of a religious turn of mind go to church, or worship God in their own way. There are plenty of people who do this in an extremely lukewarm manner, if at all. Such people, in this country, could be called lukewarm Christians (or perhaps lukewarm Jews), but they could hardly be called lukewarm Moslems or lukewarm Parsees. Though they may never go to church or synagogue, they have accepted values, ways of thinking, and ways of behaving that come from either church or synagogue. They partake, in some manner, in a certain religion, without being as it were energetic proponents of it.

Consider Mr. A. I shall not give his name, beyond saying that it is one of those names that are probably, but not necessarily, Jewish. When I go to Mr. A.'s house, it often happens that many of the people I meet there are Jewish. He is not orthodox, or in the least pious. I doubt if he goes into a synagogue from one year's end to another. Nevertheless he does not work on Yom Kippur. Occasionally, in talking to Mr. A., I have used one of those expressions that are so common that one forgets their Biblical origin, only to find that Mr. A. did not react to it: the quotation came from the New Testament, and Mr. A. knows nothing of this. He does not noticeably read the Torah or the Talmud, but he has some idea of what is in these writings (more than I do). Very likely I miss certain subtleties in his speech, too. It would not be surprising, when dining at Mr. A.'s house, to find a friend of his who would chant the ritual prayers before meals. It would not be surprising to find in his house some trinket with the Star of David on it. At Christmas time he does not have a tree in the house. In a word, Mr. A. is Jewish. He feels himself identified with the Jewish people. Jewish history is *his* history, and he can feel extremely proud of the record of his people, so many hundreds of years with a minimum of aggression, and yet so many times uncomplainingly on the receiving end of cruelty and persecution.

Consider Mr. B. His name is Smith, Jones, Robinson, or the like. He is not anti-Semitic, and at his house I sometimes meet Jewish people, but less often than at Mr. A.'s. Of the other characteristics of Mr. B. I am less able to speak, because I belong to his culture myself, and it is almost impossible ever to notice the distinguishing traits of one's own culture. But it would not be surprising if there were among his guests a minister, who would say grace before the meal. It would not be surprising if his wife, or his daughter, had a pretty necklace with a cross. At Christmas time he always has at least a small Christmas tree. Mr. B., for all that he never goes to church from one year's end to another, is a Christian.

Mr. A. and Mr. B. are *culturally* Jewish and Christian. But what is a culture? Or what makes a given culture to be *this* way or *that* way?

It is doing no more than recognizing the facts to see on the one hand that a religion (however we may come to define one) is certainly an individual matter, but that also any given religion forms and molds a certain attitude to life throughout a whole group of people.

Now the Russians certainly have their attitude to life formed and molded by—something. So do the people in other Communist countries. One speaks of "Communist country" in exactly the same manner as one speaks of "Christian country" or "Moslem country," and we may notice that there is the same incompatibility. Would it be too much of a stretch to say that communism is a religion—or at least an irreligion?

But we practice in this country a policy of religious toleration, and since we cannot tolerate communism, we conclude that it cannot be a religion. (If it were we would have to tolerate it.)

We practice religious toleration in this country the easy way, for we do not have any markedly different religions. We have two branches of Christianity, and we have Judaism. There is some friction between Protestants and Catholics, but it is moderate in amount. There is some friction between Christians and Jews, but this is greatly to the discredit of Christians, who ought to be able to understand Judaism better, since Christianity came out of Judaism and completes it. But if we had in this country a sizable population of fanatical Moslems, that would be a different story indeed.

The prevailing climate of opinion in this country, both as it is at present and as it was historically, is Protestant Christian. As for the very large number of Protestant sects, they barely differ in anything more than the form of church organization and the style of the hymns that they sing and the prayers that they use. Considering them as an influence that forms and molds a certain attitude to life, they are all but identical. To live among mixed Baptists, Methodists, Presbyterians, Congregationalists, Episcopalians and others requires no strenuous exercise of the virtue of tolerance, and we should not pat ourselves on the back or give ourselves airs for doing it.

It happened not so long ago in this country that there was a religious group, of a fair size and with considerable coherence, whose customs were markedly different from those of

Judaism or any kind of conventional Christianity. The Mormons in the West were enjoined by their religion to practice polygamy. Any trace of tolerance towards this aberration would be hard to discover, and Mormon polygamy had to go. It disappeared completely, and Mormons now practice monogamy except for a few "fundamentalists," who, only a few years ago, were arrested and brought into court with quite unnecessary crudeness and force.

We have in this country, then, only a few religions, which differ, comparatively speaking, rather little. Other countries have much more serious problems. In 1948, when India gained her independence, Mr. Nehru apparently had the naïve idea that the entire subcontinent could live harmoniously together, practicing a religious tolerance resembling that in the United States, or in England where he was educated. But no. The result was not quite war, but a violent upheaval, in which not one country gained independence, but two, India (what remained of it) and Pakistan. This entailed one of the largest mass migrations in history, even in recent history, in which mass migrations have become almost commonplace. Literally millions of families tore themselves up by the roots, placed all their few possessions on a cart or on their own backs, and endured the miseries and uncertainties of travel and resettlement. They were Hindus who would do anything to escape being ruled by Moslems, and Moslems who would endure equal hardships to escape rule by Hindus. This was on account of the utter incompatibility between the Hindu group of religions (or should it be called one religion, or a super-religion?) and Islam. We, who find tolerance so easy to practice in our far simpler set-up, must realize that this sort of thing is what a *real* religious difference leads to.

Religious wars are not only the sort of thing that happened way back "in those days"; they are quite capable of happening now.

That communism, wherever it becomes dominant, molds the character and institutions of a nation or an entire country, is clear. But even in Russia, not everyone is, technically speaking, a Communist. The Communists, the members of the party, are the elite. They work extremely hard at it, and if they rise to high positions in the party, it is they who make all the important decisions. They correspond to the active churchgoers, the pious, the fanatics. But ruthless measures are taken to insure that *everyone* has the same relation to the Communist party as the non-churchgoing Christian has to the Christian church. Everyone must accept the fundamental values, and adopt the *mores*, prescribed by the Communists. It is either that—or else.

The aims of communism are universal. *All* men are to be Communists. Indeed, they believe that all men would realize this, and would at once arise and free themselves from their chains, were it not for the capitalist press, which is not free (as Communists understand "freedom") for it is the slave of Wall Street. They have to be brought to see this truth, as revealed in the writings of Marx, Engels and Lenin (but not Trotsky or Stalin). It is always to the advantage of "the people" (this phrase never means the whole people, only the downtrodden masses) to be liberated by force of arms, and even then they often, as happened in Hungary, are so misled as not to realize that the Communists *always* have the best understanding of what is a truly progressive policy, through their study of dialectical materialism.

Hitler, at the height of his infamous career, once declared

that "nothing can stop me except an explosive idea." He was right. Quite often, when expressing huge generalizations like this one, he was extremely intelligent. By dint of an heroic effort on the part of the Western nations and of Russia, he was stopped, but the explosive idea was not in the West. When he was foolish enough to attack Russia he was doomed, for there an explosive idea had been operating in men's minds since 1917. These "explosions" are on a slow time scale. The Communist idea is still in active eruption.

What sort of ideas are explosive? Is it not true that religions provide ideas of such vividness that they are often explosive? Islam is always potentially explosive, as in Africa right now. So is Christianity, but in a different way. At any time in history there might arise—there may recently have arisen—a new, explosive religion.

But, in spite of certain resemblances that may thus be drawn between communism and various kinds of religion, it has a character which, *in our way of thinking,* is utterly shocking for a religion to possess. This is its insistence on uniformity throughout the State. For, as we see it, the State must *not* concern itself with the religion of its citizens. The State must treat anyone's religion as his own private matter. Each individual will make his judgment (or no judgment at all) as to how he will worship God, and his choice must be treated as an entirely indifferent matter by the State. And this, we are inclined to think, is a necessary character for any religion, that it must accept an equal status with any other religion, and must keep out of the hair, as it were, of "politics."

This is one of those subjects in which we are entirely culture-bound. It is the more difficult to escape from the restricted thinking imposed by our culture because of the fact that our culture is, at the present moment of world history, so tremendously dominant. A brief glance at history will show us that a number of religions, on many occasions, have by no means accepted a status of equality with other religions. A glance at the present might light upon Saudi Arabia (to take an extreme case), a Moslem country, in which there is no trace of religious freedom.

Thus the Communist religion (if it be one) is not disqualified from being a religion on account of its intolerance, even though it practices this to an extreme degree. It demands *total* adherence. Not everyone need be a member of the Communist party, but the individual *must* accept the Communist scheme of values. And this acceptance is *total* among the whole population.

But of course the Communists do not have a religion, but a most definite anti-religion. They stamp on religion and make fun of it, very energetically, for their own prophet has told them, "religion is the opiate of the people" (and there is a certain amount of truth in this!). In the very early days of the Revolution, they organized a Museum of Atheism. Needless to say, there is no religious instruction in the schools, but there is a constant stream of irreligious instruction or, as we would call it, propaganda. There is also a steady stream of what we would call indoctrination, but which they call instruction in dialectical materialism. Contrary to what we are likely to suppose, Russians are *not* badly educated. They know nothing about the West, but their ignorance could hardly equal our own abysmal ignorance of Russia-in-Europe and the whole of Northern Asia. And they all have at least a smattering of dialectical materialism. This has taught them to have an utter derisive contempt for any "belief in God." Nor do they believe in a hereafter or in spiritual forces or beings of any kind, or in any supernatural power, or in any divine order wielding sanctions against transgressions of the moral law, or even in any kind of moral law except their own kind, which is based firmly on materialism.

This is where we change the meaning of a word. Or perhaps we should start a new word, to include all religions and also this particular kind of irreligion which is (1) universal in its claims, (2) incompatible with other religions, and (3) productive of a certain flavor, a certain character, in any society where it is dominant. Perhaps we think too narrowly of a religion as a certain type of relationship with God. Perhaps we should widen the term to include *any* system of values, any organized way of thinking about what things in life are *really* important, any coherent set of fundamental beliefs which, when held strongly by a small number of the population, and accepted, perhaps passively, by the majority, will mold the character of the entire society. We may realize that such fundamental beliefs very often take the form of a belief in God, but not always. For we have on the one hand that extremely spiritual religion, Buddhism, which has no formal god, and in which the aim of every man is to escape from involvement in material things, and on the other hand we see a large fraction of the land surface of the globe dominated by a fierce and positive atheism and an intense involvement in material things. What is a religion and what isn't? In default of any new word (perhaps someone will be able to suggest a good one), let us expand the old one and speak of "the atheist religion" (an attitude toward God of some kind, if only a negative attitude), the religion of dialectical materialism, the religion of Russia and of China, of about one-third of the population of the entire earth.

New religions are apt to be explosive. The rise of communism is by far the most explosive thing that has happened in recent years. Only why did it rise? *Why* is it that there are such huge Communist populations now? If the people were all "enslaved" by Communists—who was it did the enslaving? Couldn't a billion people resist slavery?

This is one thing that our prominent anti-Communists cannot explain. They do such an energetic job in declaiming to us, quite truthfully, all the things that are wrong with communism—its utter destruction of personal freedom, its ruthless use of force, its "double think," its permanent reliance upon informers, that they cannot explain why there is any communism at all. One would think that communism had been forced upon people by some ruthless and alien visitors from a distant planet. They cannot explain that communism was planned, waited for, and finally put into execution by men, and that these men are not greedy self-seekers, avid for power or personal possessions, but are dedicated men, with a tireless, selfless, monomaniacal devotion to "the cause." And if communism were all that and only that which our anti-Communists say it is—how can it be explained that there is a "propaganda war" and that we are in danger of losing it? *Pure* evil never won a propaganda war. There must be something that, rightly or wrongly, truly or speciously, *appeals* to people. For appeal to people it certainly does—particularly if those people are starving.

Communism proposes to redistribute the wealth of the world. This has considerable appeal to the "underprivileged," to those who live, overcrowded, in hovels and wake up every day hungry and go to bed hungry. What is the appeal to them of political equality, of equality before the law, if there is no equality of the stomach? A slogan like "free enterprise" is cold comfort to anyone who lives in a drafty tenement in the winter, or in a shack in a disease-ridden slum in the tropics at any time. Even if it is true that free enterprise is the best way to maximize production, the Communists claim that they will maximize production even better by putting everyone to work, and furthermore that they will distribute the results of work properly by rewarding only those who work, and not those who merely own. In the non-Communist way of doing things, there are two reasons for having money (and money is the token whereby one has a claim on useful products, that have been made by work). One is having worked; the other is having a lot of money. In a Communist country no one can claim that society owes him caviar and champagne because his grandfather made a lot of money. There is no production "for profit"; there is only production "for the public good." And to achieve this, millions of dedicated Communists throughout the world are willing to slog away in the party machine, attend endless evening meetings, undermine and destroy liberal groups, change with all the meanderings of the party line, swallow the stale nineteenth century oversimplifications of Marx and Engels, lead a double life, working in constant danger, and, in many cases, go to prison, and often suffer torture.

Poverty is a terrible evil. Communists are determined to do something about it. With us, although we agree that poverty is deplorable, the intention to do something about it could hardly be called a fanatical determination. With the Communists it is—it is something that, as we have seen, in many ways resembles a religion.

But why *this* sort of religion, this parody of a religion, this complete antithesis of any way of worshipping God, which consists instead of a vehement and scornful denial of any god? Communism as a religion is so far from developing any spiritual values that it insists on material values, material values, and nothing but material values. And yet it is not the religion of Mammon. The worship of Mammon truly is a private matter, undertaken by some persons only, who understand only worldly goods and seek them only for themselves. The Communist seeks material values for *everyone*. "Arise, ye victims of starvation. . . The Internationale will save the human race." (Communist hymn.)

Communism is something new in the world. But, like other things that are new, it is not composed entirely of brand, shiny new ideas, freshly delivered from some idea factory. It is a combination of component ideas, most of which are probably not, by themselves, new at all, and it arose at a definite period in history, and it incorporated, either directly or by reversal, ideas that had been held previously.

The official answer to any question about the "historical origins" of communism is that Marx got his ideas, by reversal, from Hegel. From Hegel comes the dialectic, the inexorable procession of thesis, antithesis, and synthesis, which Marx and Engels took over lock, stock and barrel. Only Marx considered that Hegel had been standing on his head, and the odd turn that he gave his philosophy was considered to be standing it on its feet. For Hegel was a Platonist, who thought that Ideas were the ultimate reality—floating around in some Ideal World of their own—and that the ordinary "world" that we think we live in was just a dim reflection, or imperfect realization, of these Ideas. There was a good deal to be said (supposing this philosophy was to be adopted at all) for turning the dialectic into dialectical materialism, and actually recognizing the solid world of things.

But Hegel had no passion for reforming the world. He was entirely content to subside on his professorial chair and think Great Thoughts. Even Plato had somewhat more social concern; as a specialist in justice and ideal government he was twice given the opportunity to put his ideas into practice by governing a city (he failed each time). The later Platonists had no social concern at all. The noblest of the Greek and Roman philosophers, preaching wisdom and justice as the highest aim of mankind, preached a solitary wisdom, and resignation as the best counsel for the "underprivileged." Even the Buddha, contemplating human misery under the bo tree, came to the conclusion that all misery is caused by desire and that the aim of man is to eliminate desire. The passion for making the world a better place, for doing things for *other* people, certainly has no sources in antiquity.

Karl Marx saw the children working fourteen hours a day in the textile mills, the women, stripped to the waist, working like draft animals in the mines, and was filled with what was altogether too rare in the nineteenth century (and also in the twentieth, and in all other periods)—righteous indignation. The student of the history of ideas may remark smugly that "Marx derived from Hegel and Feuerbach" and leave it at that. But this is not the slightest explanation of the real driving force of Marx. Forgetting, for the time being, that Marx and his followers are prepared to work by means of ruthless coercion and callous deceit, that they deliberately make things worse because they believe that things must get worse before they can get better, that they use hate, not love, to generate the emotional steam for their program for the world, that in their practice (if not in their explicit statements) the end justifies the means—forgetting all these *means* and focusing attention on their *ends*—what can be the origin of this new "ism" in the world that can inspire such intense dedication and fanaticism?

There is an answer to this question in something that is, in one way, so remote, and yet is so obvious, so clear right in front of our faces, that it is difficult to see it. What else preaches "do things for your neighbor" except Christianity?

Of course Karl Marx was not a Christian; he was Jewish. But he lived in Christian countries, Germany and England, and he saw the contradiction (as he himself would express it) between the pious ideals of the Christians and their inhumanity in face of the barbarous conditions in their factories.

Just as the equality of man comes from Christianity, so (but less directly) does the doctrine of "raise thy neighbor's material standard of living—by force." Christianity began long before Karl Marx, but it is always potentially explosive, and it is always capable of throwing off temporarily explosive heresies in the most unexpected times and places. In an extremely wide sense communism can be called a Christian heresy, a heresy which denies Christ, but nevertheless accepts some part, distorted, of what is distinctively Christian. It rejects the first and great commandment "Thou shalt love thy God . . ." but enthusiastically accepts a strange modification of "Thou shalt love thy neighbor as thyself," a modification in which "love thy neighbor" becomes "see that he gets enough to eat," but is combined with "hate the enemies of the proletariat, and denounce thy neighbor if he thinks counter-revolutionary thoughts."

A historian of some distant future age, looking back and writing the history of the twentieth century, may find it in accordance with the *mores* of his time to describe all wars as religious wars. Like us, he will find past ages bafflingly hard to understand, and he will find the people of the twentieth century unspeakably strange in that, when engaged upon a perfectly clear and justified religious war, they were unable to see it. For he will understand our twentieth century war better than we do.

Epilogue

"There is much in Christianity that is common to us Communists. Only I do not agree when He says when you are hit on the right cheek turn the left cheek. I believe in another principle, if I am hit on the left cheek I hit back on the right cheek so hard his head may fall off."

—Nikita Khrushchev, in front of the cathedral at Rouen, March 1960.

7 : *Who Gets What?*

It must be a source of great satisfaction to a worker in a Russian factory to realize that, of the total wealth created by him and his fellow workers in the productive system of the U.S.S.R., *none* goes to shareholders—to men and women who make a living simply by "owning" something and clipping coupons.

It must be very stimulating to be a Russian scientist working in regular industrial or agricultural research (for the majority of scientists, there as well as here, are by no means working out more fiendishly effective bombs and missiles, but are simply in "bread and butter" research, making improved products, or manufacturing known products more efficiently). The Russian scientist knows that any improvement that he is able to make is applied for the benefit of *everybody*, not just the owners of a "private company."

On our side of the Iron Curtain things are very different. We have a "peculiar institution." It amounts to a state of affairs in which a person, simply by "owning" enough money, can attract more money to himself, in a steady, continuous flow. A person is paid for being rich.

172

One might suppose that this circumstance would have a depressing influence on the morale of workers, and of scientists, in the non-Communist world. Perhaps in many cases this is so. But it is also noteworthy that in many cases it is accepted with equanimity, even with enthusiasm.

The idea that money breeds money is accepted, of course, with great ease and complacency by those who are on the receiving end of it. It is remarkable how well it is accepted even by those who are not. The institution is known as "free enterprise"; it is made out to be a great virtue, and our children are indoctrinated with it in school.

If free enterprise is combined with genuine equality of opportunity, then it should be possible for anyone with ability to accumulate money to the point where it begins to breed more money—that is, to become a capitalist. This is something that is not appreciated by Ivan in the U.S.S.R., whose information about the West coincides not with reality but with Marx. He is told what ought to be true about the West according to dialectical materialism, which teaches that at this "late" stage of capitalistic development all the wealth is in the hands of a very few, the rest being toiling, dispossessed proletariat.

Our capitalist system has not worked out the way Marx said it would, with more and more wealth being concentrated in the hands of capitalists who grind the faces of the poor, and this is why Russians, when they come over here, seem so extremely out of date. Their ideas about the West—which are preconceived notions, resulting from their indoctrination, and are utterly impervious to reality—have a musty smell of the nineteenth century. Actually we have a pyramid, from a very few persons at the extreme top down to a broad base of people with a very modest income. There are said to be about forty people whose personal fortunes exceed $100 million. Income-tax reports show that there are on the order of 250 personal incomes "$1,000,000 or over" (244 in 1958, 257 in 1959). This compares with the $5000 (approximately) which the "average" U.S. family has to make do on. But when one compares the income brackets $5000 to $6000, $6000 to $7000, $7000 to $8000, and so on, the number reporting in each group gets slowly and steadily fewer and fewer; there is no sharp cut-off between "rich" and "poor"—there is simply a steady gradation.

Real estate and oil are about the only ways to become *extremely* wealthy in this country. A wise provision of our tax laws, not wishing to discourage exploration for more oil, decrees that money arising from the sale of oil from a man's property shall be taxed as a capital gain at only 25%, rather than the 90% that he would pay in the highest level of ordinary income tax. Such a man also enjoys a very convenient "depletion allowance." The *very* rich, then, are living by owning. They just had the luck to "own" the right piece of land, and the law says that who owns the land also owns all that is under it.

Below the million-a-year level of income the distinction between living by owning and living by working already becomes less clear. There are some fabulously highly paid executives. About two dozen of the very highest paid, presidents or chairmen of huge corporations and a very few vice presidents, receive $300,000 or more in salaries and cash bonuses. A few others reach this figure if account is taken of "deferred earnings," a gimmick which protects their tax structure. There is no denying that these executives work for their money. Great executive ability is extremely rare, and it commands in the market as high a price as all that. Not that it necessarily follows that what these men contribute to the general welfare really *deserves*, in any ethical sense, to be rewarded quite that highly. It is just that any company wishing to obtain the services of such an executive has to offer him that much, or he will go elsewhere, the demand for him is so great, and he could easily make huge sums by going into business for himself. And so what a top executive receives in the way of annual salary counts as living by working; he does something useful for it. But he is sure to have stacked away quite a lot of money which is drawing interest, and thus, in addition to the income that he works for, he gets money which is obtained just by owning money.

Further down in the tax brackets things become even less clear. A man who has worked all his life for a moderate salary, and then retires to live on his savings, can scarcely be accused of being an idle parasite. A rich playboy, who inherits his father's or grandfather's fortune, can certainly be accused of exactly that. There is also in this country much invested money that is well distributed and that by no means supports a few young men or women expensively in idleness, but adds something to the income of sensible, hard-working family men. So that in the broad middle-income range there are some who work for every penny they receive, and others who work for their pennies, but also are lucky enough to receive modest amounts of living-by-owning money. And of course there are the "underprivileged" whom we tend to forget.

If we can overcome our indoctrination to the point where

the spectacle of people being rewarded with money simply for owning money causes surprise, then we can ask ourselves the question: How much of the total money goes to people who have worked for it, and how much goes as interest on investments? Economists who have studied this question say that the proportion is about eighty of earned money to twenty, or perhaps less, of unearned money. And so, suppose someone were to say, "From now on let all living-by-owning disappear! Let no one receive money for any other reason than by working for it." How much would this amount to? According to that estimate every $80 would go up to $100. Anyone earning $8000 would find himself earning $10,000; a migrant farm laborer or a sharecropper family trying to exist on a cash income of $800 would find the figure going up to all of $1000. And this would not amount to inflation. There would be no rise in prices because the *total* purchasing power would be just the same. And it would be done by taking money not only from the rich, but also from many people in quite modest circumstances who have small investments, and those who have retired to live on their carefully put-by savings.

Similarly, if we carve up the rich, irrespective of whether they have "worked" for it or not, and distribute their income among everyone, the result averages up to a disappointing figure. If we take the 250-or-so million-dollar incomes, how much do we get? Since this bracket is one million dollars *or more,* it is hard to say. The total might be of the order of a billion dollars. Divide this among the 50 million families in the United States, and each family gets $20—they could buy a small radio, with enough over for a nice visit to a ball game. Cut off at an income of $100,000, and about $4½ billion becomes available—nearly $100 for each family. Now let us make a really drastic cut! Let us take the richest one-half of one per cent of the population, and divide their money up among everyone. Fully $30 billion would become available. Divided among nearly 180 million of the population this would give as much as $170 for every man, woman and child in the country! And yet this would be a most drastic cut, for it would take in incomes down to about $20,000, which is by no means *rich* according to our standards, just comfortable and doing nicely thank you.

But there is another side to it, another way of looking at these arithmetical figures, that makes some attempt to raise them above mere jottings on an economist's scratch pad and to clothe them with just a little human meaning. What is a dollar? What is a hundred dollars, or a thousand for that matter? A dollar is worth different things to different people. To a very rich man, a hundred dollars is as nothing. To a prosperous middle-income citizen a hundred-dollar bill is not a thing to be given to a beggar or used to light a cigarette with, but if he *should* lose $100 (he might lose it betting on a horse) the loss is not very great. If a very poor man gains $100, his gain is tremendous. If he picks up one dollar, it makes a decided difference to him. The true, human value of a dollar, its value to a human being, depends on the number of other dollars that human being has. If we were to strip the very rich down to a few tens of thousands of dollars a year (the income tax does a moderately good job of this) they are still able to jog along well enough. But if we could add a few hundreds yearly, or even less than a hundred, to the unfortunates at the very bottom of the income pyramid, that would be something really worth doing. Every time money is, by any means, gotten out of the pocket of a rich man and into the pockets of poor men, there is a net gain in human satisfactions.

The pure arithmetic of dollars hides the situation. The arithmetic of simple interest says that one dollar-year is worth five cents (or more if one is prepared to take a greater risk of losing one's capital). One thousand dollars for one year is therefore worth $50, and $50 for the next year, and so on. And a tidy inheritance of one million dollars permits a man to draw a steady income of some $50,000 every year (before taxes, of course) without ever drawing on the principal. And all the while, there are the "underprivileged," among whom many are so poor that $50 a year would be a decided and welcome improvement. If we can get sufficiently far away from our own *mores,* from all the indoctrination that we have received, it becomes possible to see in all this something that is decidedly curious, to say the least. Perhaps even it is unjust.

This situation has not gone unnoticed. There have been many people, some of them very influential, who have regarded it as unjust. They have even proposed to do something about it. They have even done it.

There are *two* things that can be, and have been, done about it, not just one. The extreme method, now in practice among nearly a billion people on a large part of the land surface of this planet, begins by expropriating all property from all owners thereof. This automatically eliminates living by owning because nobody any more owns any land, to receive rent, or money of the kind that draws interest. Karl Marx realized extremely clearly that the owning classes could never be persuaded to permit this change voluntarily, that the use of force would be necessary. In practice it requires the use of the utmost violence, accompanied by fraud and deceit and motivated by bitter hate.

The other way of doing things is the socialist way—using the word "socialist" in the Western sense, not as Communists use it. It aims to put interest-bearing property in the hands of the State, so that money-from-money is available to the government and is not portioned out, as in our haphazard way, to a favored few. There are many and important differences between socialism of this sort and "socialism" of the Marxian sort, or communism as we call it. It is done entirely by parliamentary means, and it does not need to be done completely, and all at one swoop, but can be done partially. The government can nationalize several big industries, and still leave other fair-sized industries and all small private enterprise unchanged. It is reversible, in striking contrast to anything that happens to a country after the Commies get in. If the people don't like socialism and prefer to go back to the old private enterprise, they can do it, by the usual parliamentary means. And they don't need to go all the way back, they can go part of the way back, as indeed they did in England, where the steel industry was first nationalized and then returned to the capitalist system. At all times it is democratic, it is responsive to the will of the people. If any country is socialist, it is because the people wanted it that way, and if they wanted to become capitalist again they could do so. Above all, it is done without hate, and this gives it its most distinctive difference from communism. Correlated with this, it does not have the explosive driving force that communism has; no dynamite, and no dynamism.

We have in the world, then, two kinds of economic and social systems, the Communist, and all the rest. "All the rest" means lumping together some rather different things that are at various points along a range, from the theoretical "pure" capitalism at one end to "pure" socialism at the other. There are no examples at the extremes, and every existing society is at some place or other in between. There is no pure socialism. There is no pure capitalism either. Perhaps the nearest approach to that extreme is the United States, but even here capitalism is restricted by numerous laws and supplemented by government operations ranging from the post office to price support for farm products. We have capitalism diluted with streaks of socialism. Some say it is creeping. They call it "creeping socialism" in order to make it sound as bad as possible. But socialism is voluntary, and democratic; if we *really* wanted to, we could reverse the trend and go back nearer to pure capitalism.

Our modified capitalist system works exceedingly well (with certain reservations). It is the wonder of the world. Russians, who are told that the United States is in the last stage of capitalist decadence, are also told that their number-one objective is "to overtake and surpass the United States." This is at least a compliment to the productivity of the capitalist system as we have it, even if it is true that the profit motive rules and that production is not undertaken for the purpose of satisfying human needs, but purely for the purpose of increasing the profits of the capitalists.

Successful as it is, our capitalist system has several serious, built-in inefficiencies.

Our system of free competition demands triplicating, or more, every facility. Huge organizations (they are called "private" organizations since they are outside of government control) exist for the purpose of satisfying the public demand for goods, services, everything. Their *primary* purpose is to make money for the shareholders; Ivan is right in saying this, even though he does not see, because he is not told to see, that the only way to make money is to supply something that people actually want and can be induced to part with money for. But our system demands several organizations, not just one, for fulfilling every demand. The obvious inefficiency of this leads capitalists to form mergers, trusts, combines, cartels. But our laws sternly forbid this. In order that we may receive the benefits of competition, there must *be* competition, and this means that *every* facility must be duplicated, triplicated, or multiplicated.

Is there a supermarket in your neighborhood? If it is run by, say, the Great Atlantic and Pacific Tea Company, soon there will be next door to it an entirely similar outlet run by First National, Safeway, Grand Union or Piggly-Wiggly. Often there are three such outlets, all very close to one another, all performing with the most beautiful efficiency the service of getting the merchandise into the hands of the customers or, rather, into their cars. All are provided with the necessary space for exhibiting the goods, the refrigeration, the check-out lanes and the shopping carts (many of which are idle part of the time), the cash registers, the storage space, and everything else that is necessary. This must strike our rare Russian visitors with extreme surprise. They order things more rationally in the U.S.S.R. In that great country, if it is necessary to provide a retail outlet for a "populated place" of 1000 people, or 10,000 or 100,000, they build precisely one retail outlet. It is true that they do not build it big enough, and there are always long waiting lines at the "Gum" stores. It is true that the goods available are drab in quality, by our standards, for they do not have our sensitive mechanism of supply and demand for finding out what people actually want. But at least they do not indulge in our wasteful practice of building everything several times over.

In our large cities the number of banks is quite extraordinary. Each of several competing banking companies strives to provide a banking facility within a moderate distance for everyone in the whole city. Adjacent banks, or banks opposite one another, are quite common; three banks within a stone's throw can often be seen. A bank is an expensive establishment. The premises are often in a high-rent district, the décor would put to shame an opulent temple in ancient Greece, and a necessary piece of equipment is an exceedingly expensive, massively constructed safe-deposit vault. One result of this is the well-known benefit of competition; banks are competitive, and to get customers they have to provide efficient service, and aim for a satisfied customer. Great efficiency, therefore, results from all this competition. But it is obtained as an end product of extremely wasteful duplication.

It is the same in less visible aspects of our productive system. An example: there is a process in the chemical industry which produces two products, caustic soda and chlorine. There is a demand for both of these products, but not always in the same place. A large chemical company will have quite a number of facilities for producing these products, well distributed among the locations where there is a demand for them. Orders will come in for caustic soda in this place and for chlorine in that place, and they are not always in balance with the production; it may be necessary to produce a large amount of chlorine at one of the company's plants to fill a local demand, leaving the co-product, caustic soda, to be transported elsewhere. An intricate and important task carried out in the company's main office is to decide how much production at which plant, and how much transportation, most efficiently fills all the orders and maximizes the company's profits. And since there are several large companies all performing this function, the central staff, deciding what shall be produced where, is entirely triplicated or further multiplicated.

It is the same in other departments of any large company. Research departments are multiplicated, with overlapping everywhere. If a break-through in fundamental research is made by one of the university scientists, or perhaps by a Russian scientist, everyone knows about it soon enough. But there is plenty of less high-brow research and development work to be done before the new invention is "reduced to practice." The Russians put a team on the job, and do it only once. In our economy each of the competing organizations in the field puts its own team of scientists on the job. They work under pressure, and the speed with which they arrive at practical results is altogether admirable, but meanwhile a totally excessive number of scientists are tied up in this work. The Russians are able to deploy their scientists more efficiently.

We also systematically make the wrong decision in regard to automation, or the use of machines generally. Our system inherently creates "technological unemployment" and doesn't know what to do about it. The problem has plagued the

Western world since the industrial revolution. At that time it took the form of the "looms per weaver" controversy. Increased mechanical efficiency made possible looms that practically looked after themselves, so that instead of one man per loom, or per two looms, it was only necessary to hire one workman for four looms, or ten, or twenty. Those who were dropped from the payroll as a result of this naturally disliked it; the Luddites destroyed looms in their intense anger. Throughout the nineteenth century, and the twentieth century so far, the same type of problem has constantly arisen, from one invention after another, since every invention for more efficient manufacture amounts to a "labor-saving device," and no member of the labor force wishes to be the one who is "saved."

Every time there is a new labor-saving device or invention or machine, the problem presents itself to some executive in terms such as this: His subordinate technical men have brought him all the figures, and they might say, "It costs us $150 a week to do this job, $100 in labor, $50 in other costs. If we install the new machine we can let one man go, and then the costs, including running costs for the machine and full amortization and depreciation, will be $80 for the machine, plus the $50 other costs; total $130 instead of $150." So the executive fires the man and buys the machine because he sees that the total costs *to the company* are less with the machine than with the man. The money saved by the company may be passed on to the consumer in the form of lower prices or paid to the stockholders in increased dividends or distributed among the remaining employees (from the executive down) as a raise, or perhaps added to the general reserve of the company, or ploughed back into the business. And everyone says that this adds to the efficiency of our wonderful productive system.

Everyone, that is, except the man who is fired. If he is extremely lucky, and if the labor market is just fine for him, he may be able immediately to get some other job in the same town. But it is far more likely that he will not. He may be able, while unemployed, to draw some money from the state or federal government to help him keep going; he might get $50 a week for nine months. At the end of that time, if he is lucky, he gets another job. But it is by no means unusual in our rich country for a man to become unemployed for a long period. Whole districts become full of chronically unemployed, who have to be given relief or they would just starve. Some may be able to find new employment by moving, with family and home, to a distant place. Who pays for the move? This comes out of the man's own pocket, whereas his unemployment allowance and state or federal relief are paid for out of the taxes, that is, by everybody. So that, when one considers the total welfare, it is by no means the simple "$150 a week by manpower, $130 by machine" that the executive used as the basis of his rather simple decision. Taking into consideration just the $50 unemployment allowance (never mind the man's moving costs, if any) then the balance, *as far as the whole community is concerned,* reads "$150 by hand, but with the machine $130 plus $50 for the man's relief, total $180, for perhaps thirty-nine weeks, and only after that any saving at all." It is by no means clear whether that labor-saving machine really pays for itself when one takes the entire community's interest into account.

If we lived in an imaginary world, in which no one ever had any difficulty in finding a job—and a job right in the same town—so that being fired would always be quite a minor incident, then we could say that that executive really made the right decision. But we know that this is not so. Executives are making decisions of that kind all the time, every day. Every time, they balance cost by hand against cost by machine, taking the cost *to the company;* every time, they install the machine if the balance shows any distinct advantage *to the company* on those figures. Almost every time the discharged "hand" needs financial help, from some source or other, before he is placed again in another job, and so if the balance had been made on a total community basis, instead of a company basis, quite likely that machine should not have been installed. It costs the community (not the company) *more* to install the "labor-saving" machine than to do without it.

It is not an easy matter to calculate the point beyond which further automation does not pay, but since companies calculate it, from their point of view, to a very fine hair, and since they always leave out the costs to the community of relocating the man who is laid off, it is clear that they always go beyond the true point of maximum efficiency. And this is inherent in our system; it is one of our built-in inefficiencies!

This is the reason for featherbedding—the fireman who is carried on a diesel locomotive although he is (theoretically) not needed, the live musicians whom theaters have to hire in this day and age of excellent canned music. Since the companies drop too many men, through overautomation, the unions insist that they be kept on. The basic idea is in the right direction, although the unions tend to overdo it, to balance the overdoing on the other side.

It is the same with more complex decisions than just to automate or not to automate. Shall a company abandon an old plant on the Eastern seaboard and build a new manufacturing plant nearer to the raw materials in Texas? Many complex considerations have to be weighed and balanced before such a decision is made. The company may decide to keep some of its best workers and pay their transportation to Texas; those that are left behind *may* receive some amount of severance pay. At the new Texas site, the company may have to provide access roads and other facilities to the plant; but new schools and other municipal facilities will have to be built, out of somebody's money, and meanwhile the deserted Eastern town is left with fewer taxpayers and a mounting population on relief. The *total* costs of moving a factory from one place to another are much greater than those that are borne by the company. The company will make the move if the balance shows a profit. But since the company does not bear, and does not take into account, certain large costs that are involved, the net effect on the nation may be not a profit, but a loss.

It must be far more humanly satisfying to work on this sort of problem in the U.S.S.R. The planning work is done by dedicated party members, who are competing fiercely with one another for advancement in the huge organization. When they have to balance this against that and the other, in deciding how best to do things in the economy of their enormous country, they know that they are *not* just balancing figures against figures in order to maximize profits for the stockholders, but are taking into consideration *all* the elements of the situation, including the lives of human beings, and are making the decision in order to maximize welfare for all. Under the concrete circumstances in which they find themselves, certain special considerations have to come in. Since they are ringed about by the as-yet-unliberated capitalist world, which is always hostile, they must always bear in mind the national defense and give great weight to strategic motives. And since their government rules by force and has tyrannical power over the individual, they do not shrink from moving whole populations about for political reasons.

Yet, in spite of all these inherent irrationalities in the capitalist system, where else in the world can one find so many things, and so many kinds of things, such a profusion of automobiles, of food, of clothing, of sports equipment, of gardening equipment, of cosmetics, of soft drinks, of liquor, of paperbacks, magazines and comics, of costume jewelry, of gadgets, of everything that a person can either want or be persuaded by an advertising man that he wants? And all this is not, as the Russian theoreticians suppose, confined to the luxury of the very few, the reigning capitalists, but extends remarkably deep in the population. This is a thing that, in the whole history of the world, has never happened before.

Our enormous flood of consumer goods is not only produced, it is distributed through our wonderfully efficient retail system. And it is consumer-directed. Products, and also packages, are constantly improved until they are marvels of convenience. Cars become easier and easier to drive and to repair. Food products come ready-cooked. Even the older transportation industries, long die-hards, are in some cases becoming consumer-conscious and providing for people what people actually want. A little thing that is typical of the

American way: when shopping carts were first introduced in self-service supermarkets, people would put their kids in them to give them a ride; the carts were not strong enough to be used as baby carriages, and notices had to be put up asking people not to do this; but they did it just the same; and so the carts were redesigned to be strong enough, and provided with a special seat where baby can ride. The motto of the capitalist system seems to be, "Find out what people want, and *give them what they want.*" And all this is achieved, apparently, by *allowing* a few rich people to sit on their money, and live comfortably on the interest! It is a curious world.

But all the time we have a constant haunting fear hanging over us—depression. Or a little recession. "It is a recession when *you* are out of a job, it is a depression when *I* am out of a job"—as our wits say.

The Marxists make much of the cyclic depressions that plague the capitalist system. Since depressions took place also in the nineteenth century, Marx noticed them. In the third volume of *Das Kapital* (which was edited from Marx's papers after his death by Engels, and which hardly anybody reads) there are pages and pages of rather naive mathematics purporting to explain them. Communists believe that "under socialism" (as they express it) they do not have cyclic depressions. It is not easy to say whether this is true or not. For if there were (just suppose) any kind of "depression" going on in Russia, then (1) they would be able by concealing facts to prevent people from realizing it, and (2) the government has such complete autocratic power over the population that they would be able to *do* something about it immediately and drastically, instead of having to wait, as we do, while our cumbersome and indirect "pump priming" methods slowly fill the pipelines. It is entirely possible that the Russians have cyclic depressions just as we do—either in the same cycles or in a different timing of their own—but they deal with them differently. But the Russians all think that they cannot have depressions, for these are supposed to be a necessary product of capitalism, not of "socialism," and they are convinced, for they have read it in all their books on the subject, that the capitalist world is plagued by the utter instability of its built-in depressions. Perhaps they are right.

Immense productivity, and cyclical depressions—is it worth while? If you average out the depressions over a considerable number of years, then *on the average* most of us do well enough. A person who in the course of his lifetime weathers several depressions without undue distress and achieves prosperity during the "ups" of the cycle, has little to complain about; he averages out all right. The situation is tolerable for anybody whose "downs" do not take him below poverty into destitution. But there are a great many people who, during the depression part of the cycle, have a very rough time of it. During the intervening periods of business prosperity they can get jobs, and while this lasts they are better paid and have a higher standard of living than any other workers in the world. But is this worth while for the very lean times they have to go through while the capitalist system is undergoing one of its mysterious depressions? Who wants to be an average?

Worst of all, even the "ups" of our system are not entirely satisfactory. It ought to be that, while we are having a period of prosperity, *everyone* should be able to live reasonably well, even if some, while they are sweating out a depression, may have to comfort themselves with the thought that a time will come when they eventually may be doing not so badly. Full employment, at least part of the time, would seem to be a minimum requirement. Yet we fail in even this. Even in our best and most prosperous periods, we still have unemployment, and among those who are technically "employed" there are some, such as migratory and seasonal farm workers (two million of them), whose standard of living is a disgrace to us all. We can produce, produce, produce— we always have a *surplus* of food, a situation unparalleled anywhere else in the world—but it seems we cannot feed people who are hungry because we cannot get the "purchasing power" into their hands. They do not have the money, and the capitalist system (as the Communists never tire of pointing out) will never do anything unless there is money in it. Our system demands that approximately one-fifth of the total purchasing power is to be given to people who have done nothing to earn it, and some of these people have far more than enough to satisfy their minimum needs. It certainly is a strange world that we live in.

Over at Nikita's they have licked the problem of unemployment. They forcibly put everybody to work. If there is regional unemployment, they simply transport a whole lot of people to some other region. They have arrived at the stage of "socialism," or "from each according to his ability, to each according to his work," and production is never for profit, but only to satisfy needs. They have not yet succeeded in establishing the proletarian revolution over the whole world (as was Trotsky's idea, in accordance with the original plan of Marx and Lenin) so that for the time being they have to co-exist with the still remaining portions of the capitalist world, and this necessitates a tremendous effort for national defense—and offense. Were it not for this, they would, they believe, soon reach that point in dialectical development where "the State withers away," as Marx put it, characteristically using the present tense for the future in the manner of an Old Testament prophet.

One of the beliefs of dialectical materialists is that, with them, there is no disagreement between theory and practice, whereas the world of the capitalists is shot through with "contradictions"—discrepancies between their theory, which says one thing, and their practice, which does another. It is believed that the advantages of "socialism," or manufacture for human need rather than for profit, must be so transparently clear to everyone that no one, except for an exceptionally degraded hang-over from the old regime, could possibly desire the return of capitalism. And yet in practice it does not work out this way. The State shows no sign at all of withering away, and severe, vigilant police power is necessary to prevent the return of private enterprise, of which there is a surprising amount in Russia today. Much of it has to be tolerated. *Time Magazine* (December 12, 1960) cites the statistics that private gardens limited to one acre in 1959 "turned out 46% of all the meat, 49% of all the green vegetables, 49% of all the milk, 65% of all the potatoes, and 80% of all the eggs consumed in Russia. The excess above home consumption is sold in the network of officially tolerated produce markets to which Russian housewives turn when goods are unobtainable in state stores." Occasionally such activities surpass the bounds of tolerance. A recent newspaper report told us of one of these private gardeners who raised watermelons; he was able to sell these in a keen seller's market and made an extremely sizable profit. He was jumped on, of course (theoretically he should have let the government cut itself in for a large percentage). But meanwhile the people got their watermelons! In China, too, it is reported that they now find they have to permit a considerable amount of individual agriculture, which for them is a step back from their "great leap forward." It seems that private enterprise, not to say capitalism, inherently does tend to creep back again, whatever dialectical materialism may say about the agreement between theory and practice. In Russia and China it seems they have creeping capitalism. Ever so often someone finds that there is a demand for something and that he happens to be in a position to satisfy the demand, and he yields to the incentive of the profit he can make from people who are entirely willing to pay his price. Officially this has to be rationalized by saying that such persons are "reactionary elements"—another feature of "socialist" vocabulary; people they don't like are never people, just "elements."

In our country we have unemployed—not only a large number of unemployed in hard times, but some unemployed even in the best of times—showing that the system is certainly not perfect. But then, those who have abolished our system altogether find that it comes back of its own accord, which would seem to show that at least something in it is natural and agreeable to human nature. But it has to be modified. How? We discuss the rights of labor and the rights of capital. We discuss the question endlessly. And uselessly.

It is to some extent a false question. The terms "labor" and "capital" present a false antithesis. For labor is people. People have rights, and therefore one can speak of the rights of labor. But capital is *not* people. Capital is money; it can be concisely defined as "spare money." The expression "rights of capital" is a loose, strictly incorrect expression which needs clarifying before any clear thinking can be done. Capital is not people, but it is *owned* by people, and so one can speak of "the rights of people who own capital." A person owns money; perhaps he owns so much money that some of it is "spare money," or capital. What *rights* does this give him? Does he have the *right* to demand that more money be paid to him simply because he already owns a lot of money?

This question is an extremely ancient one. It has been debated for centuries. Since it is a moral question, it has been debated by moralists who, many centuries ago, fully discussed and explored the question of "usury." They were agin it.

But what is "usury"? Since the medieval thinkers were agin it, modern thinkers have supposed that "usury" must mean "excessive interest," which we often call "usurious interest." For the moderns can hardly believe that the medievals were actually *against* interest. Yet they were.

St. Thomas Aquinas expresses it in terms that can be paraphrased thus: if you borrow, say, a man's coat, you actually *use* the coat. If you borrow a spade to dig in your garden, you *use* the spade. It would be entirely right if the owners of these articles were to make a slight charge for the wear and/or tear. But if you borrow $100 to tide you over until pay day, you return $100 exactly, and you have not used up or destroyed or consumed *anything* belonging to your friend. The hundred dollars is first taken away, and then returned intact, precisely and unchanged. The loan of money, then, has no inherent right to be rewarded with money.

But what if there is a risk of losing the lent capital entirely? Does this justify interest? Perhaps so, but only in a small amount, proportional to the risk. If a man had numerous sums of money out on loan, he would be justified in charging just enough interest to cover his bad debts, and so he would not get any richer. It has even been suggested that a rich man's dividends are his "reward for abstinence," but this is a piece of hypocrisy. If a man owns a million dollars or more, he deserves no reward for not spending it all at once.

The Church—that is to say, the Roman Catholic Church —has always been against interest. And since our modern capitalism is deeply rooted in the lending of money at interest, the Church cannot be blamed for the evils of capitalism or credited with its successes. The Church has never supported the right of money to gain more money without using itself up. But failure to support is not the same as actively to condemn. When a man lends money, to be returned in full later, it is permissible for him to charge interest for the loan *if* the circumstances are such that there is something else he could profitably have done with the money if he had held on to it. In the modern world these circumstances *always* obtain. And so the lending of money at interest is not sinful. It is not like, say, obtaining money by fraud, which is of course always sinful. It is simply a peculiar, and not entirely justified, by-product of the artificial circumstances under which we live.

The institution of money-for-money, or interest, flourished mightily once it was given free rein. It led to capitalism. It led to a productivity in material goods the like of which the world had never seen before. And it led to crisis after crisis after crisis. Our crisis has several components, but certainly one of them is the question: How shall we run the productive system? Complete, no-holds-barred free enterprise and capitalism? Complete state ownership under a moderate, democratic state? Or some mixture of these two? Or complete totalitarianism?

The question is not a new one. It began when capitalism began, in the Industrial Revolution. In the first half of the nineteenth century capitalism had already led to the atrocious conditions in British mines and factories that Marx describes with such powerful, unforgettable writing in the descriptive portions of *Das Kapital*. The question became acute, in approximately its modern form, as long ago as 1848, the year of the Communist Manifesto, which begins, "A specter is haunting Europe, the specter of communism."

The Church (the Roman Catholic Church) is an extremely slowly moving organization, and it was not until much later than 1848 that it came out with anything positive (although there were plenty of negative pronouncements) concerning "the social question." At last, in 1891, appeared the papal encyclical *Rerum novarum*, which has since been read and discussed (but insufficiently acted upon) by a very large number of Catholics, but remains unknown, or enjoys at the most a very fleeting acquaintance, among Protestants and other non-Catholics. The principles of *Rerum novarum* were reaffirmed, and spelled out in greater detail, by Pius XII in his Encyclical *Quadragesimo anno* (which might be freely rendered "Forty Years Later") in 1931. And in 1961 Pope John XXIII in *Mater et magistra* emphasized the same principles even more strongly, with special emphasis on the duty that highly industrialized countries have to help the less developed countries. His Holiness emphasized, also, that this must be done without any interference, overt or covert, with the political life of the underdeveloped countries.

Rerum novarum says, in part, "All agree, and there can be no question whatever, that some remedy must be found, and quickly found, for the misery and wretchedness which press so heavily at this moment on the large majority of the very poor . . . Working men have been given over, isolated and defenceless, to the callousness of employers and the greed of unrestrained competition. . . A very small number of very rich men have been able to lay upon the masses of the poor a yoke little better than slavery itself." This is almost the language of Karl Marx!

"Speaking summarily, we may lay it down as a general and perpetual law, that Workmen's Associations should be so organized and governed as to furnish the best and most suitable means for attaining what is aimed at, that is to say, for helping each individual member to better his condition to the utmost, in body, mind and property." Leo XIII is saying in 1891 that working men should form unions. The United States for many years after that was rather backward in social legislation, and Franklin D. Roosevelt was regarded as advanced for saying the same thing in 1933!

The evils of capitalism are unsparingly castigated in this Encyclical. But it is equally sharp and uncompromising in its denunciation of "socialism." The word "socialism" at that time probably had not settled down into either of its two present meanings, the Western meaning or the Communist meaning. The "socialism" so constantly denounced by the

Popes might be described as the following heresy: "that material prosperity is the *only* end to be pursued by man." The Socialists are also attacked for their proposals with regard to property: "The Socialists, working on the poor man's envy of the rich, endeavor to destroy private property, and maintain that individual possessions should become the common property of all, to be administered by the State or by municipal bodies." The recommendation of the Encyclical is in an entirely different direction. Instead of property being more and more centralized and nationalized, it is to be more and more distributed. Exact equality (in material goods) is not even aimed at, but it is hoped that as many people as possible will become property owners.

Rerum novarum is not a complete program of action. It is a blueprint. It describes a state of affairs which would constitute a just society and which we can keep in mind as an ideal to be aimed at. It does not spell out what steps we should take to arrive at such a state, for this would be politics and outside the proper sphere of action of a church.

Capitalism says that private enterprise must be free and unfettered in order to maximize production. Socialism says that private enterprise must be strictly controlled, and in some areas abolished altogether, in order to correct the appallingly bad distribution of wealth that naked capitalism leads to. Communism says that everything must be done by the State. All these "isms," in their different ways, deal with abstract principles concerning the means of production. *Rerum novarum* gets down to the root of the matter, which is people. It says that the important thing that *must* be achieved is that a working man shall receive a *just wage*.

And what is a just wage? It is certainly not something arrived at merely by the "higgling of the market," so that in times of an oversupply of labor the prevailing wage rate goes down. And it is not just a nebulous ideal, incapable of any application as a criterion to concrete situations. The idea of the "just wage" can be explained with great simplicity and with quite sufficient precision for the purpose. The Encyclical puts it tersely: "The remuneration must be enough to support the wage earner in reasonable and frugal comfort," and it goes on to explain that the wage must be enough for the wage earner to bring up his family, and also to permit him, if he is reasonably frugal and is not a spendthrift, *to own his own house.*

The kind of society visualized in *Rerum novarum,* then, allows that there will be rich people and also poor people. Christians should need no reminding that our Lord Himself has told us that the rich will enter the Kingdom of Heaven, if at all, with far greater difficulty than the poor. But Leo XIII did remind us of this, and also of the constant duty of Christian charity. *Anyone* who is capable and willing to work should be able to receive the just wage, and only a bum or a ne'er-do-well need fall short of "reasonable and frugal comfort." No society that fails to achieve this can for a moment be considered satisfactory. "His [the employer's] great and principal obligation is to give to everyone that which is just. Doubtless before we can decide whether wages are adequate many things have to be considered; but rich men and masters should remember this—that to exercise pressure for the sake of gain, upon the indigent and destitute, and to make one's profit out of the need of another, is condemned by all laws, human and divine. To defraud anyone of wages that are his due is a crime which cries to the avenging anger of Heaven . . . Finally, the rich must religiously refrain from cutting down the workman's earnings, either by force, fraud, or by usurious dealing; and with the more reason because the poor man is weak and unprotected, and because his slender means should be sacred in proportion to their scantiness."

Is there a chance of achieving a society as described in *Rerum novarum,* or a reasonably close approach thereto, in the world today? We see in the world many different kinds of economic systems and a vast range of prosperity, from countries where many of the people are abysmally poor up to the United States and several other countries where the standard of living is on the whole astonishingly high. In the United States we certainly do not have equal distribution of wealth. *Rerum novarum* makes no demand for equal distribution. But we have here, as of 1961, 29 million home owners. At about four persons to a home, that comes to close on 120 million people living in owned homes—a substantial portion of the population. And as for the other kinds of property besides "real" estate (the curious lawyer's phrase seems to suggest that anything other than land isn't real at all, although for money purposes all is convertible) the publicity agents of the large companies delight in reminding us of their employee stock-purchase plans, whereby their workmen can become part owners of the company that employs them. Many of them become part owners of other companies as well. As of 1960, there were 13 million people in this country, or one out of eight adults, holding stocks or bonds, and this number is said to be increasing at one million per year. These 13 million people hold investments of $350 billion, which gives an average of $27,000 per investor; this "average" lumps together everyone, and seeing that there are some extremely large fortunes, there must also be some most modest investors. Indeed, nearly fifty per cent of all investors have incomes in the $5000 to $10,000 range. And 1.3 million of them are members of trade unions.

All this stacks up fairly well against the ideal described by Leo XIII, and certainly much better than in any of the Catholic countries. We have not gone in for socialism, we have developed a sort of modified capitalism of our own—and it has worked out on the whole admirably. It does not *equal* the ideal, but it is never to be expected that such a thing should happen in human affairs. We must have ideals, but two things should be remembered about them all the time: (1) we will *never* completely achieve any ideal, and we are not doing too badly if we reach a moderately close approach, and (2) there is always the opportunity, nay the necessity, to do better.

In the classical Marxism of the nineteenth century, it was supposed that in the future (the twentieth century) the rich would more and more viciously grind the faces of the proletariat and that society would become sharply divided into two classes, the owners and the dispossessed masses. The Communists of the early twentieth century played on this. The modern Marxists in Russia, although largely glued to their stale nineteenth century theoreticians, seem to be sufficiently in touch with reality to discern, at least in a dim way, that as regards their arch-enemy the United States this is scarcely a true picture. Their propaganda line has changed accordingly. "The proletarians have nothing to lose but their chains. They have a world to win. Workers of the world, unite!" was the slogan of the barricades in 1848. But as of today, more than a hundred years later than this, colonialism has for some time been their main pitch. Africans unite (and let us help "liberate" you); Cubans and other Latin Americans unite against the Yanquí; Asians, turn against your oppressors (and Hungarians, remember you belong to *us*). The emphasis seems to have changed. It is no longer strictly economic; a large element of race consciousness seems to have come in.

Yet has it changed? It is an element of Marxian theory that economics, in the last analysis, controls *everything*. Perhaps another look at our economic system is in order. Our modern capitalist system has produced, *in the United States,* a state of affairs having an appreciable resemblance to an ideal, just society. But capitalism is not a system working only within the borders of the United States and a few other highly industrialized countries. It spreads everywhere; everywhere, that is, except where the Communists have been able to exclude it, and to set up their own system. What happens to the capitalist system when it crosses over some of those "Lines on the Map"?

To the south of our country is a long line, part of it the course of the Rio Grande, part of it an arbitrarily assigned parallel of latitude, separating us from our Good Neighbor, the Sovereign State of Mexico. At designated places there are throngs of Mexican "braceros," eagerly competing for the privilege of leaving their families for months at a time to work on our farms, under horrible conditions, for wages that should put us to shame. We have laws to prevent more than a limited number of Mexicans from entering this country as seasonal farm laborers. But then there are "wetbacks," who defy our laws and swim the Rio Grande, so frantically do they wish to get away from economic conditions in Mexico.

No one seems to think of applying the principles of *Rerum novarum* to Mexicans.

The Belgians seemed to suppose that, after they had precipitately granted independence to the Congo, they would continue to receive "their" revenues from the vast mines of copper, uranium, cobalt and industrial diamonds in Katanga, which contributed over $200 million annually to the Belgian economy. As it turned out, the loss was so serious that their standard of living had to be noticeably reduced, a painful operation which led to much bitterness and was accompanied by a severe general strike. It is clear that the standard of living of the Belgians had been too high all along. They should have shared some of their wealth with the Congolese. They were exploiters, in the classic Marxist tradition, only the exploitees were of a different color from the owners. Even more drastic will be the effect on Portugal, a much poorer country than Belgium, when the inevitable happens in their huge colonies, Angola and Mozambique.

Nobody likes an absentee owner. The situation has occurred constantly throughout history, classically in the form of the absentee landlord. Thus, in Ireland, at the time of the potato famine, the land on which the peasants worked was theoretically "owned" by Englishmen, to whom rent was due. The rent was a fixed sum, famine or no. Thus it came about that throughout the famine Ireland was exporting potatoes to England to raise money to pay the rent. (It may be noted that *some* of the English landlords "forgave" the rent during the famine years.) Our industrial society, considered on an international basis, is riddled through with absentee ownership, not only in agricultural products, such as sugar, but in the mineral bases of our industrial system, copper, tin, and petroleum, to mention only three very controversial items.

An American enters the factory of an oil company or an automobile company, where he is employed. He does his work and receives his pay check. He knows that the product is sold for a sum substantially exceeding the raw-materials-plus-labor cost of making it and that the profit (after taxes) is distributed among the shareholders who own the company. And who are the shareholders? Quite likely he himself is one. Or maybe he has an aged aunt who is living cozily on her late husband's savings, which have been prudently invested by an insurance company in a well-diversified holding, including shares of the company for which he works. He knows also that some of the profit that his labor helps to create goes to a few people who have acquired immense fortunes from oil or automobiles, but then maybe his son has won a scholarship from one of the foundations that these people have set up. And so this person may not listen with much enthusiasm to a Communist who tells him that he is being exploited and that this is a crying shame.

It is very different, or at least it was very different, for a man who worked in Cuba. At certain times of the year he would be able to work on the sugar plantation, hacking the canes down with a machete—monotonous, physical work requiring muscles and endurance but a minimum of skill. The canes disappeared into a factory, where they were converted into the crude sugar of international commerce. For this he was rewarded with a wage, but no one could possibly say that it was a *just* wage. Support him and his family in "reasonable and frugal comfort" and let him (if he was thrifty) own his own house? Not for Pedro in the sugar fields!

If Pedro were well informed, he might know that the United States paid for his sugar a price decidedly in excess of the "world market price." But if he got this information from some more sophisticated Cuban, that person might go on to tell him that the excess in price that the United States paid would all go back states-side again in the form of dividends on its immense investments in Cuba. What with United States companies owning sugar plantations, and owning this and owning that, the extent to which Cuba was owned by Yankee outsiders is hard to imagine. When Castro went on an expropriation binge, he seized, up to early in 1961, about $1.5 billion of assets. The interest on $1.5 billion, at probably well over 10 per cent, makes a tidy sum yearly, and Pedro never saw a bit of it. It is true that a considerable sum in dollars came right back to Cuba again in the tourist trade. But this money never went far from Havana, and that portion of it that went to Cubans ended up in the pockets of grafting politicians, hotelsters, gambling-joint operators and pimps. It is pleasant for the United States housewife to be able to buy sugar at only fourteen cents per pound, but it is not just. The price of sugar is altogether too low.

And so it turns out that the capitalism that we enjoy is naked capitalism after all. Any modifications we have been able to graft onto it, to prevent the extremes of exploitation foretold by Marx and deplored by Leo, are for ourselves only, and have not been for export. The Russians do well to denounce "colonialism." They are most active at the United Nations in demanding an immediate end to colonialism. But it must be remembered that Communist tactics have not changed since the days of the Scottsboro boys. A peaceful, prosperous and independent Africa, as we understand "independence," would be by no means to their taste. Africa is of more value to them in a state of turmoil—until they can come in and "liberate" the entire continent.

Communists have always utterly opposed living by owning and the "exploitation of man by man." They see, for it is only too clear, that there is plenty of exploitation in the world today, but it is largely on a country-by-country basis. The industrial countries exploit the less developed countries of the world. The Belgians exploited the Congo, after a brutal conquest, under the political forms of colonialism. But we exploited Cuba (and other Latin American countries) just as effectively under the *appearance* of the utmost political independence and freedom for the exploited country.

A gigantic task ahead of us is to build up the prosperity of most of the rest of the world. We do it partly by loans of staggering size, $78 billion since World War II on various economic and military aid programs, and partly by investments—for example, $2.8 billion in Venezuela, $800 million in Brazil, $700 million in Chile, and so on. President Kennedy has called for an increase in private investments abroad, for these countries need irrigation dams, power plants, fertilizer factories, steel mills, textile mills, etc., which cannot be built up without capital in huge amounts. But we ought always to insist that the countries into which we pour money have strong labor unions, to make sure that the workers receive something approaching a just wage. Otherwise, the money tends to stay in the hands of the rich and the corrupt, to make them richer, and the amount of "trickle down" is most disappointingly small.

Wherever we have exported capital, we demand our interest. For we take it for granted that money breeds money, and to us a foreign investment of a million dollars should "return" well over 10 per cent, perhaps $200 thousand every year; an investment of a billion dollars, $200 million yearly. And we complacently suppose that foreign countries will continue to pay us these dues. But they may not. Those who invest in foreign countries would be well advised to take into account the possibility of losing their investments.

We must export our prosperity, or die. For if we do not export our prosperity, then assuredly other countries will export their revolutions. To bring prosperity to other countries we must export capital. But we must not export capital*ism* unless we are able to mix it with a considerable dose of *Rerum novarum,* or of anything else bearing some resemblance thereto. We must find some way of getting capital into underdeveloped countries without necessarily demanding the full pound of flesh that the capitalist "system" permits. If we do not, then all the investments we make abroad are helping to build up the Fidel Castros of tomorrow.

8 : *Love, Money, and a Little Heresy*

"And the moral of that is—'The more there is of mine, the less there is of yours.' "
—The Duchess in *Alice in Wonderland*

FOR MANY THINGS IN THIS WORLD, the more there is of mine the less there is of yours. For all the hard, thing-y *things,* that is true. But it is not necessarily true for the intangibles, which have ways of their own.

For real estate, it is obviously true. There is only so much land surface on the globe, and the more there is of mine the less there is of yours.

For love, not only is it untrue, but the contrary is true. Love has this very remarkable thing about it, that the more there is of mine, the *more* there is of yours.

How does money rate in this regard?

At first sight, it seems to be clearly a more-of-mine-less-of-yours kind of thing. If a man robs me of $100, or if I pay him that sum for anything, there is that much less of mine and exactly that much more of his. All our commercial transactions are based on this. "Annual income twenty pounds,

208

annual expenditure nineteen, nineteen and six, result happiness. Annual income twenty pounds, annual expenditure twenty pounds, ought, and six, result misery" as Mr. Micawber put it. Money seems definitely to be among the thing-y, tangible *things*.

But money is not so tangible as all that. Coins and bills are tangible, but all the cash in the United States certainly does not amount to all the money. A man who is "worth" a million dollars does not hold that much legal tender. His "money" consists of entries in a bank's books or of scraps of paper, suitably engraved, that represent his investments. Economists have debated this matter, and one plausible definition of money is "money is as money does." The amount of money that *theoretically* represents the total wealth of the United States has no objective existence as a *thing*. For if all the rich men tried to realize their assets at the same time, the necessary amount of money just wouldn't be there. Money is partly intangible, not tangible, and it partakes to some extent of the quality of some of the intangibles that it is *not* necessarily more-of-mine-and-less-of-yours.

We spoke in the last chapter of cutting off the top peak of income and distributing the money over the bottom layers of the money pyramid. The amount gained by each person in the lowest income levels would be disppointingly small, but this would be compensated for by the enormous gratification with which he would receive it. If this change could be made, the rich would have to do without their luxuries and status symbols, but the gain to the poor would be real and important. Thus there would be a net gain in human satisfaction, even if it were a matter of taking the same pie and slicing it differently. But the actual gain would be even greater than this, for the pie would not stay the same. It would become a bigger pie. There are only two things a person can do with money, spend it or save it. The poor do not save because they barely have enough money to live on; the rich save some of their money. But if money were taken away from the rich and distributed among the poor, less money would be saved and more would be spent. This would lead to greater demand for goods, which would stimulate production, and bring many of our large supply of unemployed (to say nothing of the few who had previously been idle rich) into the effective labor force. More people would be working, more products would be made—and so the total pie would get larger. When it comes to getting extra money into the hands of the poor, the moral seems to be "the more there is of yours, the more there is of everybody's."

We all deplore the lot of the poor, and we all agree that something should be done about it. But there are two schools of thought about what to do: (1) to make the poor richer we must make the rich poorer, and (2) to make the poor richer we should make the rich richer; or rather, we should do as little as possible on the governmental level, since the rich are eager to carry out their part of the program themselves. Answer (1) says that the poor should be given a slightly larger slice, and then at the same time the pie will become larger. Answer (2), based on entirely different economic beliefs (and economics is the most uncertain science there is) says that the poor should be given a slice which is the same proportion of the whole as before, or perhaps an even smaller fraction, but this will increase the size of the pie to such an extent that the resulting yield to the poor will actually be higher. Which is right? It is hard to know anything for certain in economics, but it is at least logically possible that *both* are right. It could be that each of these procedures would increase the pie. And that is the one thing that these divergent views of economics have in common—they both recognize that the size of the pie isn't constant, it can be increased. And so, what is money like? Is it in the class of thing-y *things*, like real estate, or does it show some resemblance to love, happiness and a few other intangibles that are not subject to the rule of you-grab-or-I-grab?

It may be that money makes the world go round, in a certain sense. Love makes the world go round in a much higher sense. It may be that money is not entirely grubby and grabby. Perhaps, to some extent, it follows the saying, "Give, and ye shall receive." It certainly seems to follow the saying, from the same source, "Unto him that hath shall be given." It seems, at least at times, to be connected with love, when one considers the saying, "For where a man's treasure is, there shall his heart be also." But is it connected with happiness? No one seriously doubts the connection between love and happiness. We have a popular saying, "Money does not bring happiness," but it is hard to say with what sincerity we believe this. Altogether, money seems to be by no means a direct antithesis to love. And certainly they are by no means incompatible. It is possible to achieve money *and* love—and what more could anyone want than that?

One acquires money either effortlessly by inheriting it or by diligently pursuing it. In this respect money is like knowledge, scientific achievement, artistic skills, and many other such things (except that for these inheritance alone is never enough). Someone once asked Newton how he discovered the law of gravitation. He replied, "By thinking about it all the time." If anyone had ever asked Beethoven how he achieved eminence in music, his answer could scarcely have been different. When we consider anyone who has managed to amass a really large sum of money, we do not need to ask the question, for it is clear that he thinks about money, if not literally *all* the time, at any rate with a large and successful share of his attention. If we consider any of those wonderful people who manage to give, and therefore receive, a large measure of love in all directions, it is not necessarily true that he or she has consciously thought about love in the manner of a mathematician or of a philosopher trying to pin down the absolute or confine the abstract. But it has not come entirely without effort. A person who has achieved this has tried to achieve it; tried and succeeded. Such a person has deliberately, and with conscious effort, not allowed the pursuit of money or of anything else to interfere with the outpouring of his (or more usually her) warm and affectionate heart.

Everybody wants love. Everybody wants money. Perhaps there are a few exceptions. There do seem to be a few solitary self-sufficient people, who give no love and receive none. Naturally, they are not likable people. With regard to money, there certainly are exceptions and in varying degrees. There are many who are decidedly lackadaisical about pursuing money (maybe they are lazy) and there are a few who, once their minimum demands are satisfied, have no interest in doing anything to obtain any further sums of money. And it is to be noted that those who have no interest in money are apt to be among the happiest of people, whereas those who attempt to do without love are morose and miserable.

The demand for love is universal and insatiable. There can never be enough of it. And since it is a more-of-mine-more-of-yours kind of thing, there is nothing except our own cussedness to prevent the total amount of love in the world from increasing without limit. Psychiatrists have now discovered love. Formerly, under Freud, they had only discovered sex—which needed no discovery anyway, only Freud found it in the most unexpected places, under every bed as well as in it. Every juvenile delinquent is traceable to a bad home environment, a broken or unhappy marriage, father on the bottle, perhaps mother (as well as father) in the hay, poverty (often but not always), bad home management, neglect—adding up to what the psychiatrists coldly describe as "parental rejection," which means that the poor kid doesn't get enough love.

When the United States Government kindly makes a loan of x million dollars to such-and-such a country, in order that it may purchase (from the United States) a tidy force of M-60 tanks and F-104 planes to fight off the neighboring Communists, who are threatening to come in to raise the standard of living among the ignorant peasantry—there is very little love in the transaction, only fear. Our huge loans for agricultural and/or industrial development are decidedly better. For example, we have undertaken a most ambitious program of aid to India, designed to increase that country's production. The purpose of this is to feed Indians since at present far too many of them never get enough to eat. There is also a notable program directed toward the same objective in South America. This was initiated by President Eisenhower in the last months of his administration and may be considered a result of the prodding that that complacent president received from the revolution in Cuba. Thus the immediate motive had a considerable element of fear, but there is far more love in feeding people than in arming them. Other industrially developed countries of the west have similar programs of aid to the underdeveloped countries. A country that has been notably active and successful in doing this is Israel, which has supplied capital and technical assistance for numerous projects in African countries and in Burma. In many cases this is being done under the immediate driving force of fear—fear that the Communists will get there first and do it better. But it is being done under the remote driving force of the Christian and Jewish religions, in which God is love. For the Communists the driving force is stronger, and much more direct, for with them religion, politics and economics are one and the same thing—but are *not* based fundamentally on love.

But love is individual. Ambitious projects to dam rivers and build hydroelectric power stations, start steel plants and tractor factories, introduce the use of fertilizers and develop improved methods of agriculture—all these things from their very nature cannot be done on a basis of individual love. Love enters into them at the very best only in an indirect way. Other motivations, fear, greed and pride, are terribly likely to be present too. President Kennedy eliminated these motivations, in calling for volunteers for the Peace Corps, by offering them *no money*, only the local wage scales in the countries where they will work. He also ingeniously brought the word "peace" to work on *our* side. The Commies have popularized "peace-loving" this and "peace-loving" that to such an extent that "peace" had almost become a dirty word. But with typical Communist contradiction they call on their followers to "fight for peace." Our Peace Corps will work for peace. Our dollars will be followed by individuals, and with love.

It is the same in race relations, in our own country or elsewhere. Love must provide the cure for bad race relations, and yet no one can love a whole race. The Southerner shouts "nigger lover" at the liberal, and sometimes the taunt is justified, for there are white people who are so super "liberal" that they try to love Negroes on a racial basis, which is entirely wrong. The Southerner can point to the old state of affairs (before the Northern and "Communist" agitators) when the faithful old Negro on the plantation or in the household was treated with genuine love. This is true, for a state of slavery, or near slavery, is not incompatible with love. But slavery with love is not the right state of affairs, and very often it was slavery without love, which is the worst possible combination. With every improvement in civil rights and social equality the white Southerners find themselves reacting with a sort of shocked horror, for they feel that their ability to love is lessened. This is what fills them with such genuine anger and sorrow. The next step, which is so difficult for all of us, and has been partially achieved by some, is to look forward to a state of affairs in which there is a possibility of love together with equality. We look forward to equality in a legal and social sense (not necessarily economic equality) without any regard to skin color. But although equality will be for everybody, love will be as it is now, a highly individual and personal matter. No white succeeds in loving all whites, and no Negro loves all Negroes. In the very distant future of this country, this division of people into "whites" and "Negroes" will be obliterated. Long before this happens, we must be able to think of people simply as people, whatever their complexion, and love as many of them as we possibly can.

How many kinds of love are there? For though we can love many people, obviously we cannot love them all equally or in the same manner. There are specialized loves and generalized loves. There is the generalized love of friendship, which is not limited as to number. There is the specialized love of parents for their children, and of children for their parents. These are reciprocal, but not symmetrical; *two* kinds of love are involved, which have different qualities. There is the highly specialized love whereof Venus is the goddess. It is uniquely individual, and non-transferable. It is, of course, intimately connected with other things, such as sex and reproduction. It can be more intense than any other love. Perhaps for these reasons it is more liable to become twisted. For there are twisted loves of all kinds, and more in the specialized loves than in the generalized love of friendship. All these loves partake of the true quality of love to the extent that they are infused by charity; that is to say, all love is a reflection or refraction of the love of God. Charity has been accurately and poetically described by St. Paul in his famous chapter, I Corinthians 13. And there is even that highly specialized form of charity which is tax-deductible. It is just a little better than no charity at all.

What is the opposite of love? As Aristotle says, the opposite of a good is an evil, as "the contrary of health is disease, of courage, cowardice, and so on. But the contrary of an evil is sometimes a good, sometimes an evil. For defect, which is an evil, has excess for its contrary, this also being an evil, and the mean, which is a good, is equally the contrary of the one and of the other. It is only in a few cases, however, that we see instances of this: in most, the contrary of an evil is a good."

The opposite of love, clearly, is hatred. Yet it does not seem to be *quite* opposite to love. Love is inherently and unqualifiedly (that is, *absolutely*) desirable. But one cannot quite condemn hatred in the same unequivocal terms. Certainly in the kingdom of heaven there will be no room for hatred, but on this earth we cannot give hatred a blanket condemnation, under all conditions. There are some things on earth that we must hate; it is our duty to hate them. We must hate evil wherever we see it. But we must hate the evil, *not* the evil person. Hatred should never be hatred of people. The simple rule is: "Love the sinner, but hate the sin." In one particular context this would read—love Communists, but hate communism. It is very easy to state, but most difficult to carry out.

Hatred, like love, has inspired some fine poetry. Probably the vast majority of great poems and novels are based on love, but there are some notable exceptions. When T. S. Eliot writes of Mr. Prufrock and Sweeney Agonistes, it is with no love, but with a considerable dose of hatred. D. H. Lawrence in all of his works expressed a strange mixture of love and hatred—for they are miscible, in certain proportions and perversions. Kafka was a poet of hate, and of fear. Samuel Butler was a great hater. So are all Angry Young Men, in England or elsewhere. Shakespeare expressed some bitter hatred, for example in *Troilus and Cressida.* In Communist writings, as is to be expected, hatred is rife. Sometimes it is personal, as in their stinging polemics and pitiless denunciations, but in *Das Kapital,* Karl Marx, writing no more than factually about nineteenth-century British industrialism, expressed some of the sharpest and finest hatred to be found anywhere in literature. And there are perversions of hatred, as there are of love. A literary example is in *Moby Dick,* where the great sin of Captain Ahab is that he hates a whale—a mere animal.

Intermediate between love and hatred is indifference. There is nothing to be said for, and very little about, indifference. It has never inspired any poetry.

But there is another intermediate between love and hatred, of a different kind, and this is tolerance. It is certainly not plumb in the middle like indifference. It seems to be nearer to love, since it is far, far removed from hatred. It also has affinities with indifference. And yet, in some ways, it is a different kettle of fish from all of these.

No one could say of tolerance that it makes the world go round. At the most, it prevents the world from splitting when it attempts to go round in different directions at the same time. Some cultures and civilizations use a large quantity of it; others, hardly any at all.

In our own culture, which is so continually changing that change has become part of the culture itself, there is very much more tolerance than there was several hundred years ago. In that distant epoch from which we have emerged people were so intolerant as to have religious wars. Do we have fewer wars now? (Our wars are certainly far more destructive, but that is a separate matter.) As we have seen, we are engaged right now, coldly, in a religious war, but we have disguised it to ourselves as a political war, as if politics and religion could ever be completely separated, even in our culture. Over there, among our enemies, they are identical.

The State *is* the Church, for the State has swallowed the Church (except for some indigestible remnants of Christianity, which are reported to be remarkably viable). We practice a large amount of tolerance amongst ourselves. But we cannot tolerate Communists, and we do not even attempt to.

Tolerance works like this: if I say something, and somebody contradicts me, we simply agree to disagree. Nothing could be more straightforward, more civilized, or apparently more rational. If we disagree about something like the merits of Michelangelo, or how to mix a Martini, this is very easy. If we disagree on something important, such as theology, politics or economics, it is not easy. Each has to say to the other, "You are entitled to your opinion." And certainly we are. In our civilization, as of the present time, we have achieved wonders of tolerance, and we can indeed be proud of ourselves for our success in this eliminating, or greatly reducing, many causes of friction. It is moderately easy to say to a man who disagrees with us, "You are entitled to your opinion." We may be able to say to a man who flatly contradicts us, "You may be right," but we must realize that this necessarily implies, "And I may be wrong." It is not easy to draw this necessary conclusion. It is far easier to relapse into an attitude which seems to say, "You may be right *and* I may be right." When we take this easy way out, we are saying in effect, "This may be true *for you,* but something else is true *for me.*" This is the Relative Heresy, and although its motive is kindness, it results in a victory of tolerance over reason. For reason tells us that, if ten people make mutually incompatible statements about the same subject, then (assuming that it is some subject on which the truth could conceivably be ascertainable, in some manner, i.e. that they are not ten meaningless statements) either nine of them are wrong and one right or all ten are wrong. To believe otherwise is to abdicate from reason.

Everyone wants to be loved. But here a striking difference appears. For who wants to be tolerated? No one. Indeed it is intolerable. If it were conceivably humanly possible to have everyone love everyone else in the whole world—a wonderfully desirable state of affairs would result; indeed, it would be heaven. A Christian is bidden to love everyone, including his enemies. He is not bidden to tolerate them. To love one's enemies is excruciatingly difficult, but just possible. But sometimes it would be quite out of the question to *tolerate* them!

Tolerance is truly a little heresy. It is little, not in the sense that few people adopt it, for it is enormously popular. It is little only in the sense that there is so much less wrong with it than with the other possibilities. It is only a heresy in the sense that it is not *quite* right. God is Love, and love together with understanding make all heresies evaporate. But tolerance, although of course vastly better than its own opposite, intolerance, is still far removed from love. There is a sense in which hatred is akin to love. But in no way does tolerance bear any resemblance to love. Tolerance is compatible with hatred; you can hate someone, and still by a great effort of will you can practice tolerance. But if you *love* someone—then all question of "tolerating" him or her entirely disappears. Tolerance is a wise, prudent repression of hatred; it is a double negative, it is a brake on the bad consequences of hatred or dislike. It has no positive powers at all. What a contrast to love! One cannot cure delinquent children by tolerating them.

In this country we have our own peculiar set of heresies. All countries do, all civilizations, all cultures. Opinions that in this country, at this time, would be taken for granted would seem in some other culture like something out of cloud-cockoo-land. If a heresy can be an opinion "contrary to the accepted doctrine on any subject," then what is a heresy in the United States could be the soberest orthodoxy by the yardstick of the general opinion of mankind, averaged over many countries and long periods of time. But we have to find this average, calling in the help of anthropologists and historians—and taking what they say with a large grain of salt. If we can find this entirely generalized, human orthodoxy, it is known as the Natural Law—only to say this is a little heresy, in our local, temporal climate of opinion. The Natural Law is known to all men *in its principles,* but in the particular precepts derived from the principles there is remarkable divergence. Our own divergences are as remarkable as anyone else's. It is up to us to notice them, and become aware of them. Nothing can be more valuable than a heresy hunt, provided we hunt for our own heresies.

Is it really a conclusion, flowing from the principles of the Natural Law, that an inconvenient, arbitrary line, decided on by treaty makers who didn't know the topography, should rule that a peninsula attached to Canada should be part of the United States? And that we must all be indoctrinated to react with the utmost vehemence against any proposal to change this? The Natural Law says nothing, in its principles, about blond-haired, blue-eyed Aryans, or any kind of skin coloration. It *does* say something, deep down in its principles, about property. It is in favor of it. We can notice the feeling for property in other people (with the exception of certain temporal and local heretics, in the U.S.S.R. and elsewhere) and deep down in ourselves we can discern the feeling for *owning* things. The Natural Law—when we can find it—is the touchstone for heresies.

But what is the cure for heresies? To a certain extent it is the Natural Law again. A people that live according to the Natural Law, and whose conclusions from its principles do not diverge too wildly, cannot be far wrong. But to find the Natural Law is troublesome and uncertain. It demands searching other peoples and other times, and searching ourselves. When found (if indeed this can be done beyond the principles) its precepts are, like all law, dry and even harsh. Something else is needed. That something else is Charity. And Charity is Love. We will always get into hassles with other people. If necessary, we can rely on tolerance to prevent a hassle from turning into a roughhouse. But we will do far better to keep tolerance where it belongs, as a sort of counter-heresy when heresies get out of hand. What we need is the strongest possible, most wonderful kind of orthodoxy. What we need is Love.

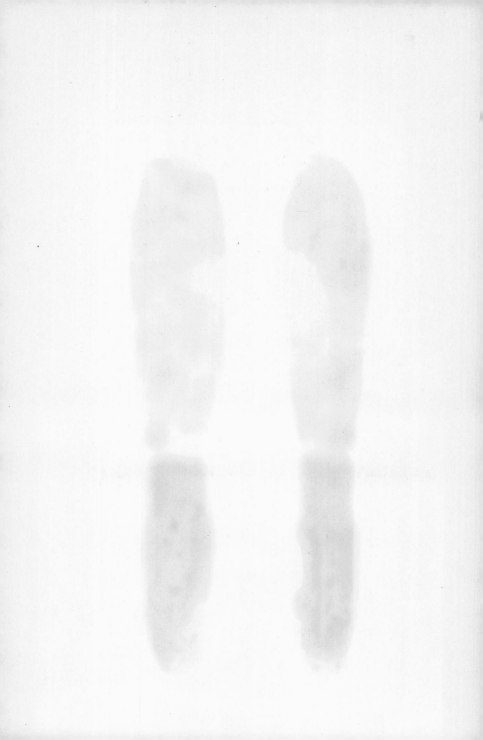